Art and Science of Whitetail Hunting

W9-DJM-814

Art and Science of Whitetail Hunting

How to interpret the facts and find the deer

Kent Horner

Stackpole Books

Copyright © 1986 by Stackpole Books

Published by
STACKPOLE BOOKS
Cameron and Kelker Streets
P.O. Box 1831
Harrisburg, PA 17105

All rights reserved, including the right to reproduce this book or
portions thereof in any form or by any means, electronic or mechanical,
including photocopying, recording, or by any information storage and
retrieval system, without permission in writing from the publisher.
All inquiries should be addressed to Stackpole Books, Cameron and
Kelker Streets, P.O. Box 1831, Harrisburg, Pennsylvania 17105.

Printed in the U.S.A.

Library of Congress Cataloging-in-Publication Data

Horner, Kent, 1936–
    Art and science of whitetail hunting.

    1. White-tailed deer hunting. 2. White-tailed deer. I. Title. II. Title: Art and
science of white-tail hunting.
SK301.H673   1986   799.2′77357   85-22088
ISBN 0-8117-2008-X

*This book is dedicated to hunters
of the white-tailed deer, especially to those
who sit in the top of trees and wait.*

Contents

Acknowledgments

First, I thank Louise for understanding in good spirit my deer hunting. Second, for line-drawing illustrations, I appreciate the efforts of Dixie Holcomb, an excellent outdoor artist, for her artistic interpretations of the white-tailed deer. Further, I thank Anthony Clifton, a young, talented outdoor writer and photographer in his own right, for photographic assistance.

Moreover, my hunting friends: Eddie Evans; Howard Evans; the McBride brothers; Paul and Andy and their sons; Dee Harper; Steve Boozer; Dr. Wayne Woods; and Terry Bush, *Esquire*, have taught me a lot about whitetail hunting.

Professionally, as a field editor for them, I am indebted to Jack Brauer, publisher; Al Hofacker and Dr. Robert Wegner, editors, at *Deer and Deer Hunting Magazine* for their help in many ways. Further, I enjoy my professional affiliation with Grady and Judy Smith, the publisher and the editor, at *The Great American Outdoors Magazine*.

Too, it would be improper should I not thank all of you at Northeast Alabama State Junior College in Rainsville, Alabama, especially Dr. Charles Pendley and Alton Hester for many stimulating and philosophical conversations about the natural order on planet earth where we and the white-tailed deer live.

I thank, too, James and Gladys Horner for their important part in this book. Upon their word, November 15, 1936, was a cold, snowy day in the hills of east Tennessee. A good day for birthing a baby.

Preface

The contents of this book should help you become a better deer hunter. In the book I've tried to give the best information available about the white-tailed deer, gleaned from both expert hunters and research biologists. In short, I believe the more the hunter understands about a whitetail, the better all-around hunter, both technically and ethically, he is.

As both a biologist and hunter myself, I have the deepest respect for the white-tailed deer and those who hunt and study this fascinating creature. Frankly, I do not pretend to be either the best hunter or biologist knowing about the whitetail — except, perhaps, around a warm, glowing campfire when tall tales start to grow after a long day's hunt. Then my stature improves, as does that of all hunters when they recount their exploits.

My intentions in writing this book are, first, to provide up-to-date, reliable information for those who are already hunters. Second, for those able-bodied souls who have thought about becoming deer hunters but have never started, I encourage you to begin. You need it, even if for the following reasons: the experience of rolling

out of a warm, comfortable bed at 3:00 a.m. on a cold winter
morning; putting on a few layers of long johns and camo coveralls;
loading your deer hunting gear into a pickup truck; rumbling forty
miles through the predawn darkness; walking a frosty trail to the
base of a mountainside tree; bolting a cold metal stand to the tree
trunk without losing your wing nut; getting in the tree stand and
inch-worming up about twenty feet, wringing wet with sweat; then
sitting there freezing for six hours or so, trying to fool a white-tailed
deer.

Now, before you condemn such insanity, let me hasten to say that
there are thousands of hunters who not only enjoy that mixture of
pain and pleasure but, further, they become addicted to it. Why?
Well, basically, I think, because man enjoys a challenge, a gamble,
and excitement, necessarily, in his quest for his meat of existence.

Moreover, many present-day city dwellers, who perhaps grew up
on farms, or their fathers did, yearn for a chance to escape the city
and enjoy a stint in the wilderness. A deer hunt provides that opportunity. Deer hunting is the opposite of anything civilized, thus
its strong attraction to the person who likes a pinch of rough-and-
tumble spice in his life.

On a muzzleloader hunt, for instance, the niceties of civilized
living are stripped away quickly when the hunter removes his white
shirt and necktie, dons his camo coveralls, and loads into the back
of a pickup truck with a bunch of bearded brethren for an all-night
ride to a game preserve three hundred miles away.

Life then becomes basic, primitive, and honest. Suddenly, directions, time of sunrise, wind, temperature, and trust in a fellow
hunter become all important. Important enough that you may
sometimes have to stake your life on them.

Yet, among deer hunters there is that subtle happy-go-lucky attitude of acceptance, acceptance of nature and life itself, and the
experiences that it brings. Moreover, deer hunting is a good physical
and mental therapy. Where else could you sit in the top of a tree
without a hospital attendant in a white jacket coming to carry you
away? While deer hunting, however, sitting in the top of a tree is
perfectly accepted. Further, you can get by with a certain amount of
refreshing uncouthness as a deer hunter.

That deer hunting helps one to appreciate that part of man's
supposedly civilized, sophisticated, plastic, glossed-over, high-

speed, ulcerated, computerized, tension-causing, nervous, political world is, at least in part, an ill-conceived, meaningless joke.

A special kind of skill is called for when the hunter is miles deep in a wilderness, alone, and he must reckon with all of the animate and inanimate forces of nature. No amount of artificiality, pretense, or civilized sophistication helps then. Here, the game must be played by nature's rules, not by society's.

Nature, in all its beauty and splendor, can be unforgiving. For example, the law of gravity cannot be defied while you are up in your tree stand; neither can you wander aimlessly through a wilderness without noticing where you are. The hunter, whether actually hunting or scouting, must constantly be aware of woodland objects, directions, and terrain. Thus, a hunting partner is quickly relied upon should one become snakebit, lost, injured, or need some ammunition, an arrow or two, a lift out of the woods, or even a simple drink of water.

It is no wonder then that a deer hunting buddy becomes an important friend. Because he is your friend, you learn to put up with his snoring, his bad jokes, his bragging, and most of his other human frailties, because chances are he has done the same for you.

Deer hunting brings together a hodgepodge and large cross section of people and personalities, and levels them. Deer hunting is a great equalizer. For instance, should you be a devout "man of the cloth," but get lost in the wilderness on a deer hunt, suddenly you become extremely thankful for any salty but precise directions out of your dilemma. Then, it matters not that your directions upon this earth came from one of lower moral degree because, at that instant, in your eyes, the helpful, bearded hunter gained the stature of Moses leading the Children of Israel out of the wilderness.

Too, should you be a rocket expert or an astronaut familiar with all kinds of space directions and lunar trajectories, you can throw it all out the window on a deer hunt. Then, you may find that the moonless night and the leaf canopy overhead doesn't even permit sight of the North Star, much less the Big Dipper. You may have to admit that, after all, you should have brought a simple compass, for you have just passed that "big stump" back there for the third time. Therefore, you're lost and are traveling in the most common of trajectories, the "proverbial circle."

I read somewhere once that Aldo Leopold, the father of game

management in this country, said he wouldn't own a son who wouldn't harvest a deer. Leopold probably said that with some tongue-in-cheek humor; however, remember that he, too, was a deer hunter.

After thinking about Leopold's statement, though, I believe that he made a valid point. Not that he would actually disown his son, but at least in spirit he would be disappointed in the lad's failure to recognize that, finally, life is based upon muscle, blood, and effort in our own survival. Early man certainly had to hunt for his meat, and it is conceivable that our kind may *have* to hunt again sometimes.

Thus, I think Leopold was saying that we should not be apologetic for being human and struggling for our meat instead of always buying it at the meat counter. Deer hunting permits us to do that, still. In so doing we may better appreciate those tribal peoples over the earth who have preceded us and given us life through their hunting efforts.

All veteran deer hunters know that the actual act of harvesting a deer is only a final link in a long chain of events. Unless the hunter is just downright lucky, much hard work preceded the moment of actual harvesting. Equipment purchase, practice, scouting, map reading, acquiring hunting privileges from the land owner, plus a host of other odds and ends ultimately figure into one's harvesting of a white-tailed deer.

Unlike any other participant sport that I know, deer hunting is bringing together college-trained scientists and the bearded, good ol' boys in one common interest. In my own case, I belong to both groups. I mention these two groups because they are a lot alike.

To start with, one has to be a little possessed to, legitimately, belong to either faction. My reason for saying that revolves around your personal discipline: the discipline to spend time in your life sitting and studying in the laboratory in the case of the scientist, and the same necessary discipline required to sit in a treetop, studying, waiting, and trying to fool a white-tailed deer as the hunter does.

Within this gap, then, I'm tossing this book, in hopes that both groups, the scientifically trained and the good ol' boys, will read it.

Chapter 1

The Deer Hunter
and His Equipment

The Necessary Hunter

The hunter is the deer's best friend in the long run. For, finally, by the hunter's best efforts, game management fees are paid, salaried game managers are hired, and herd populations are controlled at the proper carrying capacity of the land.

In the main, the combined efforts made by deer hunters, game managers, and research wildlife biologists have brought the white-tailed deer back from the brink of extinction. In the early 1900s the whitetail population reached its lowest ebb. Only about 500,000 deer were left in the entire United States. Now there are nearly 25 million. Further, the whitetail population has doubled within the last eight years.

This successful rise in the whitetail population is a tribute to the sportsmen, federal and state conservation agencies, and many citizens groups in this country.

The species destruction allegations aimed by the antihunting lobbyists toward hunters in the United States are for the most part illogical. In short, it is not the seasonal hunter but the constant destruction of habitat that ultimately decimates wild game. In the case of the white-tailed deer, when given any kind of a sporting chance, as a species they will survive.

In short, the hunter and the deer need each other. Since time immemorial the natural system on earth has been such, and the hunter-hunted relationship is no different today. In early times, man depended upon deer to sustain him and his family from hunger.

Although presently the deer hunter may buy his meat cheaper than hunting for it, there still remains that primitive need for the attempt. With his advanced technology, modern man is headed more and more toward a world dominated by paperwork and contraptions of every electrical and mechanical sort. Sadly, we are losing touch with the muscle, blood, sweat, and heritage of the frontier days that sustained our fledgling nation over many rough spots.

Too few people take the time to appreciate the rough-and-tumble, yet honest world of our frontier forefathers. Deer hunting gives us a chance to do that, still. As a deer hunter, one can go back in imaginary time and re-live precious moments from our history. They are delectable but they are not easy. That, however, is the captivating attraction to deer hunting.

For example, to sit at dawn twenty feet up a tree and peep through the lifting fog and first penetrating light rays is a primitive undertaking. Early man did the same thing in trying to harvest his food. Now, with a bow or a muzzleloader, the deer hunter can become one with the Indian or frontiersman when he harvests a white-tailed deer in this primitive manner. To read about it is not enough, however; the hunter must experience it to appreciate the efforts made by our forebears in pursuing the elusive whitetail.

Food harvested with honest sweat should not be lamented over. And the deer hunter who takes his meat with a bow, for example, should feel no moral shame in doing so. By obtaining his meat in this fashion, the hunter actually develops a deeper respect for his whitetail quarry and is more positive toward game management policies.

Undoubtedly, bow hunters, especially veterans, have the greatest respect for white-tailed deer. Many hours must be spent on stand by a bowman in harvesting his prey. The hunter feels his own pain, frustration, and hunger as he goes about this difficult, primitive endeavor. The severe quest and complete adoration of the deer finally are displayed on the hunter's wall. This quest may be one of the most meaningful events in a person's life.

Philosophically, deer hunting does play out the life-and-death drama of existence on earth. Thus, engaging in this fine sport should not be taken lightly or unsafely. Sure, most deer camps abound with guffaws, tomfoolery, and an air of lightheartedness. Yet, the camaraderie between deer hunting friends is a fast bond.

Deer hunting as a recent participant sport did not gain great public momentum as far as numbers until the early 1960s. Now, with increased transportation facilities, highways, off-road vehicles, good game management policies, research data, state and federal management areas, and private land usage, deer hunting affords nearly anyone of legal age the opportunity to hunt.

The novice deer hunter, however, will soon learn that this great American sport presents different levels of hunting, challenge, and expense. Deer hunting *is* big game hunting, but it is inexpensive enough that the average person of economic means, if he so desires, can enter into it.

Purchase of equipment gains initial importance. And, nothing says, of course, that a deer hunter has to hunt any certain way as long as his method is legal. In fact, my observation is that no two deer hunters hunt exactly the same way. Deer hunting, thus, in the end is a highly individualistic sport depending on several factors: age of hunter, expenses, time that can be spent, concept of the sport, meat for the table versus trophy racks, and several other preferences as individual as each hunter. From these come many conversations and good-natured controversies: which brand of rifle to use, caliber of rifle, powder, lure scents, camouflage, vehicle equipment, stalking or still-hunting, where to hunt, and on ad infinitum, all of which build interest in the sport.

These diversified interests are adding to deer hunting not only as a sport but as an industry. These varied activities are no doubt good for the sport. They afford people physical exertion and thus relaxation, provide jobs, mental stimulation, education, research, and a better overall understanding of our biological system and environment on earth.

The outdoor products industry then is a part of every deer hunt. Bow hunters tell one another why they do or do not prefer using

A reliable 4WD vehicle is necessary for traveling over rough terrain. Many camping hunts are made miles deep into mountainous regions. Here the author is preparing a midday meal after an early-morning bow hunt on the Cumberland Plateau in Tennessee.

During gun season, a high-powered, scoped rifle works best on whitetails. The scope enables the hunter to verify antlers at a greater distance. It also increases the hunter's chances in making a clean harvest by placing his shot within the vital zone just behind the buck's front shoulder.

bow-sight accessories; rifle hunters argue into the night over which they prefer: a high-precision .30-06 with a high-powered scope or the nostalgic preference of a "crank-lever" .30-30 with iron sights.

Then either to the approval or dismay of both groups, up walks some bearded old-timer, deliberately in buckskins, toting a flintlock or a custom-made long bow, declaring that "there is nothing like the way I do it." Thus, the individuality and peculiar challenges afforded the whitetail hunter become pleasant obsession for each in his own way.

Deer Hunting Equipment

A typical equipment list considered necessary for white-tailed deer hunting includes: 1) own or have access to a 4WD off-road

Paul McBride, an excellent bowman, harvested this spike buck and doe on the Skyline Game Preserve in northeastern Alabama. Bow hunting is top-of-the-line in hunting sport, as more advantage is given to the deer. Also, in many states, the bow hunter enjoys a longer season, and usually either-sex deer are legal.

vehicle for traversing rough, rocky terrain to get near your hunting area and the harvested deer; 2) rifle of one of the following calibers: .30-06, .308, .30-30, .270, or .243, which should have a scope for both accuracy and detecting antlers on bucks at a distance (unless the hunter prefers iron sights); 3) muzzleloader for primitive weapons hunt on many game preserves, for which the .45 and .50 calibers are popular; 4) bow, especially for early-season, either-sex deer hunts. Modern-day bows may be outfitted with quiver and sights for convenience and accuracy. The compound bow, with draw weights from about 50 to 70 that let off from one-third to one-half in resistance at full draw, are popular hunting bows. Many hunters deliberately set the draw weights at around 55 to 65 for tree-stand shooting. Here, often shooting in close, cramped, and awkward

Muzzleloader hunts are becoming increasingly popular. Here, Howard Evans is shown with the .50-caliber Hawkens rifle that downed this heavy-racked buck in southern Alabama.

positions it is advisable to set the poundage below one's maximum pull. Further, most tree-stand shots are made at less than forty yards, anyway.

5) Proper clothing preparation for early-morning deer hunts should start no later than the night before, when you check the weather forecast and lay out appropriate clothing. It is always better to don too much clothing rather than too little.

The deer hunter adage, "You can always pull it off, but you can't put it on if you don't have it," is certainly true. No white clothing should be showing unless it is snow camo, of course, since deer easily detect white objects such as another deer's white tail flag. Too, articles of white clothing may be mistaken by another hunter for a deer's white flag.

Outer camouflage patterns of tree bark, WWII, Vietnam, Tiger stripe, or snow camo are effective in deer hunting, depending on the vegetation or environmental background. Boots, socks, long johns, gloves, cap, and raingear should match the temperature and weather conditions. To stay comfortable in falling temperatures, the hunter should add layers of clothing, such as another pair of long johns or a heavier pair of camo coveralls.

6) Food and water. It goes without saying that a three- to four-day deer hunt should be sustained with ample food and water, especially water. Water becomes critical in slaking one's thirst after a long hike, after trailing a wounded deer, and in rinsing out the harvested deer. And, a chocolate candy bar for quick energy after a long hike helps, too.

7) Compass and topographical maps. A compass is a must for both safety, convenience, and valuable information while hunting or scouting. Anyone can become lost, especially after nightfall or in flat, nondescript terrain. A compass, at least, prevents the hunter from walking, unknowingly, in the proverbial circle that is so easy to follow when lost.

Topo maps aid the hunter in finding streams, waterholes, elevation contours, flats, mountains, and ravines. When walking any certain contour, ravine, or trail after dark, reflector tape is useful in following a trail that has been made previously. Reflector tape is especially useful in leading the predawn hunter to his preselected tree. A flashlight beam striking the tape shows from several yards away. For environmental and aesthetic reasons, on his return trip, the hunter should collect any reflector material that is not quickly biodegradable.

8) Flashlight and matches. A flashlight is needed for two critical reasons: a) to let other hunters know that you are not a deer walking through the woods during dark hours, and b) to keep the hunter on his own trail. Either a headlight or a hand-carried flashlight is ample for this purpose. Keep the light on for your own safety and precaution while trampling through the woods. Another hunter could mistake you for a deer during twilight or dusk hours. Matches, of course, can provide the hunter with heat and a visible signal should he become lost in cold weather.

9) Lure scents. Cover scents such as fox or skunk are used to mask the hunter's scent. They are typically applied to the bottom of one's boots with swabs or worn as a pad.

Sexual scents composed of female pheromones collected from the urinary tract of a doe in sexual heat are sold commercially. These lures attract bucks to an area during the rut.

10) Calls. Rattling and calling tactics are used by hunters to bring deer into an area. In rattling, a pair of buck antlers is carried to the hunting site. Here, the hunter clashes the antlers together intermittently to simulate the sounds made by rutting bucks battling for dominance and breeding.

Commercial calls that simulate the distress sounds of a fawn are used to entice does toward the hunter. Deer and predators are attracted to distress calls. The doe may come to protect her fawn. Coyotes, foxes, and hawks are attracted to small-animal distress calls, too.

11) Field-dressing equipment. A sharp, sturdy knife is mandatory for field-dressing a harvested deer. Before leaving on the hunt, hone your knife until you can shave paper ribbons from a newspaper page. When you can do that, you know that your knife is adequately sharpened. A sharp, heavy-bladed knife is needed for cutting through the chest cavity and aitchbone between the deer's hind quarters.

12) Tree stand. The hunter's tree stand may be one of his most important items on a deer hunt. Often many hours must be spent on stand to take a wily white-tailed deer. The hunter's own safety and

comfort may depend on his tree stand. Some tree stands are made for both gun hunting and bow hunting. Regardless of type, it will need to support your weight twenty feet or so up a tree after you have climbed to that height with the stand. Some stands are one-piece and others are two-piece. Quietness, safety, and shooting freedom are the features desired when purchasing a tree stand. Before using a tree stand, however, the hunter should check for its legality. Some states do not permit use of tree stands on certain hunts.

Deer hunting by its nature is demanding. Thus, while in the field,

A sharp, sturdy, heavy-bladed knife is recommended for field-dressing a whitetail. Opening the chest cavity and cutting through the rear quarters are the toughest parts.

tomfoolery, pranks, and consumption of alcoholic beverages are out of the question. In a true sense, the serious deer hunter does engage in a life-and-death struggle every time he goes afield. Both the life of the hunter and that of the deer are at stake. Of course, the hunter should always maximize his own safety factors when climbing, carrying his weapon, and when hunting.

Yet, fair chase, ethics, sportsmanship, and safety are important practices for the hunter, even when competing for trophy bucks. Safety consciousness is called for when using firearms and bows, climbing treacherous terrain, during freezing temperatures, when vehicle driving, dragging or carrying a harvested deer, and approaching a downed deer.

Wild boar and the white-tailed deer sometimes live in the same quarters in the eastern and southern United States. Thus, while loaded down with your deer hunting equipment, you naturally would not want to upset one of these tuskers.

Although deer are evasive, a buck in rut can turn on the hunter. There are documented accounts of people being gored by bucks. Antlers, after they harden, are lethal weapons. Thus, personally, I do not advise doe-in-rut lures being applied to one's clothing. A wounded buck, though generally reclusive in nature, should be treated with caution when cornered.

Gunshot wounds and hunters falling, however, constitute the greatest hazards. Brush shots and those made after dark are dangerous errors made by novice hunters. Hunters should learn early in their hunting careers to identify game before shooting.

Deer hunters should be aware that more and more hunters are using the rattling technique to call up deer. Thus, shooting toward the sound of antler clashing should definitely be avoided.

Tree-stand climbing can be dangerous if precaution is not taken. Metal and wood of sufficient strength must be used. It only takes one mistake to induce misery. Thus, sensible climbing heights, safety belts, and, sometimes, choice of tree are important in being safe rather than sorry.

Successful deer hunting from a tree stand, though, is best done from a height of about twenty feet. Otherwise the deer are more likely to see you. Nevertheless, the deer may see you even if you are up thirty feet or more. Members of the cat family have been preying upon deer for eons. Through evolutionary time deer have learned to occasionally look up for their own survival. Admittedly, that is not their main means of defense, but deer do survey the woodland heights to twelve or fifteen feet when they glance upward from browsing. Consequently, the hunter should be somewhat above that height in his tree stand. Also, the higher the hunter is in the tree, the better his human scent is dissipated.

On stand the deer hunter should wear camo grease on face and hands to break up his pattern. All movement should be slow, deliberate, and without noise. A metallic rattle or squeak is almost sure to alert any whitetail that is close by. Deer quickly learn to tell the difference between natural woodland noise and any intervention by man.

The Deer's Approach

Obviously, the most critical time for the deer hunter is the moment of truth as the deer approaches the hunter's stand. No amount of money spent on the best equipment and no number of hours of practice spent with a bow or gun can overcome a costly mistake as the deer approaches. Then, hitting a metal stand with a bow limb, arrow shaft, or gun butt will likely cost the hunter a deer. So, knowing *when* to shoot is the most important, yet intangible characteristic of a successful deer hunt. The hunter looks for that instant when the deer is close, broadside, and looking away, if possible. Of course, all of those conditions may not coincide, thus the terrific challenge presented to the white-tailed deer hunter. Too, those conditions may match up, but the hunter realizes that a sapling stands between him and the target zone just behind the deer's shoulders. Many a bow hunter has put it all together only to find that his arrow deflected from an unseen sapling at the last instant.

Therefore, a hunter in a tree stand should anticipate his shooting lanes prior to a deer's approach. Also, the right-handed bowman and gunman shoot much more easily over their left shoulder. Consequently, it is important for the hunter to angle his stand on the tree in anticipating this left-sided shooting zone if he is right-handed. The opposite is true for the left-handed shooter. The rifleman, however, may switch hands, but this is not so easily done by the bowman.

Finally, most successful deer hunters consider two personalities:

the landowner and the hunter's family. For in harvesting deer consistently, a great amount of time is needed in scouting and on stand. So, the landowner's providing a place to hunt, and family members who understand a hunter's long absences, ultimately, are important.

In the end, though, venison fairly harvested and prepared for the family table with one's own recipes gives a satisfaction unique to the hunter's own experience, an experience that is part of our early American heritage.

Chapter 2

Hunting Practice and Safety

Preseason Conditioning

As with any other sport, there are ways for the hunter to practice, stay in shape, and hone his skills for safe deer hunting. During the off-season the hunter may scout for new trails and practice shooting his bow and/or rifle. These three off-season activities relate directly to deer hunting when opening day comes.

Finally, then, successful deer hunting amounts to the hunter being at the right place at the right time, with the right equipment and the right skills. It takes the right stuff. In short, deer hunting involves the hunter's total person: his will, his attitude, and his dedication to the sport.

There are varying degrees of difficulty in deer hunting. Terrain has a lot to do with the stamina and endurance called for in many regions. Carrying or dragging a deer over mountainous country is very demanding, and the hunter should be in good physical condition before attempting it. The best practice I know of for staying in hunting shape is walking — lots of it. Hiking, mountain climbing, and extended scouting trips over the intended hunting area will pay off when the season opens.

The hunter should consider his age and physical condition before any hunting trip. He cannot change his age, of course, but he can improve his physical condition. Most exertive movements such as jogging, rowing, cycling, weight-lifting, racquetball, wood-cutting, and distance running are excellent exercises for conditioning. The best simulation of a deer hunt, however, is actual walking over rough terrain. Uphill and downhill walking, in which the hunter must encounter rocks, saplings, and uneven footing, requires its own special skills. This is excellent off-season practice for staying in shape. And although it may sound rather ridiculous, loading up a sack of rocks and dragging them over the ground is excellent practice for dragging a deer. A 200-pound buck gets heavy real quickly if one is two miles back in the mountains, particularly when afoot and alone. Muscles built and hardened from July or August onward come in handy while toiling with a field-dressed deer.

Shooting Practice

There are several ways that the hunter can practice and stay in condition during the off-season. In getting ready for bow hunting, which usually opens the deer hunting season, the hunter should practice not only with two-dimensional targets but with three-dimensional, life-size deer targets. Commercial manufacturers make such models from foam rubber or other lightweight, durable material.

These three-dimensional, life-size models, when placed behind natural woodland shrubs, imitate the event of a real deer that walks up near one's stand. Further, the bow hunter should climb into a stand about fifteen to twenty feet above the ground and practice shooting downward. This preseason activity does much to hone his skills: It builds arm and back muscles, sharpens one's shooting eye, conditions legs and heart for tree climbing, and, most important, the bow hunter gets used to shooting downward from his elevated stand.

The one most common mistake made when shooting downward from a tree stand is to overshoot the target area. The reason for this is that when shooting downward at an angle, arrow deflection due to gravity is less. Thus, the elevated hunter must compensate for this difference in his arrow trajectory. But as the shooting distance from the hunter's elevated stand increases over flat or uphill terrain, arrow deflection from gravity is more noticeable. These differences in arrow flight and bow handling are best worked out in preseason practice rather than on opening day of the season.

Eddie Evans, one of my hunting friends, has built an elevated platform in a tree for bow practice. So, prior to bow season, he and

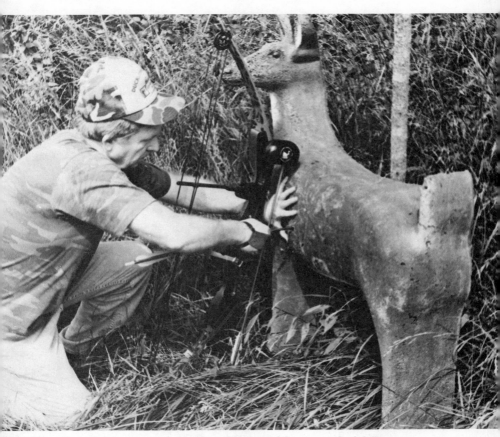

The author extracts an arrow from a three-dimensional deer target. Such 3-D targets placed in the woods get the bow hunter ready for opening day. Targets are made from durable foam rubber and can be used for lots of practice shots before wearing out. Targets should be life-size for best results, so the hunter gets used to the height of the deer and learns to quickly aim at the kill zone.

Dee Harper practices his bow shots before opening day. Here, Dee climbs into a tree stand and practices shooting downward at targets placed behind saplings at about twenty yards distant. Preseason climbing helps to keep a hunter's muscles and shooting eye tuned for bow season later.

I practice shooting from this platform at three-dimensional deer models placed behind saplings and shrubs. Most bow hunters know that saplings seemingly sprout instantly when an arrow is released and may cost the hunter a deer. A slight deflection-shot may not; but energy is lost by any arrow deflection, and penetration is less when the deer is struck.

Consequently, by deliberately placing the deer model behind saplings and shrubs in practice, the bow hunter gets used to picking his shots between and around woodland obstructions. This helps the hunter "see" a one-inch sapling before releasing an arrow. It applies directly to the time, later, when a deer walks up and a similar shot must be made.

Bow hunting by its nature is a primitive sport, and much advantage is given to the deer. However, the hunter's sense of accomplishment is heightened when he meets the wary whitetail on its home turf and wins. The deer's approach, then, is quite an important and adrenalic moment. The hunter's heart and pulse accelerate as he watches the whitetail move slowly toward the stand. To down the deer, the hunter must do everything correctly, and that includes nocking the arrow, drawing the bow, aiming, releasing, and being quiet and almost motionless during the whole process. Alas! All of this must be done while one's pulse is pounding his eardrums.

But, that is the challenge which provides the exhilaration of the moment when the hunter connects. The hunter re-lives those primitive moments — just as the earlier, tribal hunters — later, when he enjoys a venison meal with family and friends.

Well before the fall bow season, a hunter does well to select the best-constructed, safest, quietest stand from which to shoot. There are several commercial manufacturers of such stands, and the bow hunter finds that it is time well spent in selecting a stand that suits him. Tree stands can be bought from a local outdoor shop or ordered directly from the factory or mail-order supplier.

In buying a tree stand, the hunter may wish to purchase a safety belt which permits easier, safer movements while drawing a bow at an elevated position. Wherever the hunter makes his purchase, he should get used to the stand and other equipment well in advance of the season. After a few dry runs in climbing, bow shooting at a three-dimensional target, and descending the tree, the hunter will find that opening day of the season is just a similar repeat. Other-

From twenty feet up in his stand, a hunter soon learns that arrow deflection due to gravity is less when shooting downward. By practicing before the season begins, a hunter learns to avoid this common error of over shooting the deer's target zone.

While shooting from an elevated position, the bow hunter must not only learn to compensate for an altered arrow flight, he must also learn to shoot from cramped quarters. Under such restrictions, most compound-bow hunters shoot at less than their maximum pull-poundages. A draw weight of around fifty-five pounds is popular for many hunters.

The harvesting of coyotes by deer hunters is now legal and recommended in many states since coyote populations have increased sharply. Here, Dee Harper checks his arrow flight and penetration toward the 3-D coyote target.

wise, new unfamiliar equipment and nonconditioned muscles will greatly decrease the chances of bagging a deer.

In this whole procedure, however, the most critical decision for the hunter is knowing when to shoot. No amount of practice or expensive equipment compensates for an ill-timed shot. That know-how only comes with experience which is usually a combination of successes and failures. And a deer hunter relives both of those moments, the hits and the misses. The important thing is that the hunter learns from his miscues.

I shot an oak tree and two saplings with my arrows before connecting with a whitetail. But after the frustration and embarrassment subside, errors later became moments of enjoyable joking and possible hilarity among friends who, if they have hunted much, have had similar experiences.

When actually bow hunting, prior scouting should lead the hunter to the most active deer trails possible. Then, the selection of a suitable climbing tree within easy arrow range over the trail must be made. Tree species change according to latitude and elevation within the country. Where I live in the Southeast, a tulip poplar is a choice tree to climb. It is sturdy, has smooth, soft bark, and is often located near woodland deer trails. Sometimes, though, an active deer trail mandates that the hunter climb a rough-barked tree. In this situation, a close position to open shooting lanes takes precedence.

The only critical requirements are that the tree be sturdy and of the right size to accommodate the hunter's tree stand. In my region, shagbark hickories are also common in woodland flats. Thus, my shooting position over the trail sometimes requires that I climb the shagbarks. On this hickory species the bark is hard, rough, loose, frayed, and difficult to climb because the bark catches on the side bars of the tree stand. When climbing such trees, care is required, else the metallic sounds made by the tree stand alert the deer that may be close by. Spare parts, such as tree-stand bolts and wing nuts, should always be carried when the hunter starts his climb.

It is a frustrating moment, indeed, to carry all of your gear deep into the woods and start to climb, only to lose a wing nut or discover that a spare is not available.

Several deer hunters now participate in three different firearms seasons: bow, muzzleloader, and high-powered rifle. Practice techniques similar to those I have given for the bow hunter also apply to the gun hunter. The exception is that the gun hunter should shoot toward other types of targets placed among woodland shrubs. Two-dimensional, life-size, paper deer targets work well for this. It is just as important for the gun hunter to practice climbing and zeroing-in his muzzleloader or high-powered rifle as it is his bow.

For instance, the muzzleloader hunter should practice recharging his gun while sitting twenty feet up in his tree stand. It is often quoted that during frontier days, the best and fastest woodsman required about a minute to recharge a muzzleloader after firing it. But sitting twenty feet up in the air in a cramped position in a cold, biting wind, you will probably take much longer than that. The correct amount of powder must be poured down the barrel. Then the lead bullet must be started with a bullet starter. Next, the bullet is packed down against the powder with the ramrod. Last, the firing primer is placed on the nipple, and the muzzleloader is ready to fire again. Likely, by then your appreciation of the frontiersman's hardships will have greatly increased. As with any other acquired skill, the muzzleloader hunter may soon become quite good at this hunting technique.

Furthermore, the buckskin clothing and other pioneer equipment that the present-day deer hunter may wear and use adds to deer hunting enjoyment. Not only in the mind's eye but in actuality, the hunter may then closely approximate the emotional atmosphere surrounding an old-time deer hunt.

The high-powered rifle hunter with more precise equipment has a better chance at harvesting deer, provided that he gets the shots. Such popular deer rifles manufactured in .30-06, .308, .270, .30-30, and .243 calibers are all excellent in harvesting a white-tailed deer. A scope mounted atop the rifle is useful for both antler detection and accuracy. With a high-powered, scoped rifle, the deer hunter can attempt shots that would be difficult or impossible with a muzzleloader or bow. However, even for the rifle expert, time spent in shooting from an elevated tree-stand position during the preseason is not time lost when opening day arrives.

Safety and Precaution

Safety on any deer hunt is mandatory. It goes without saying that no drawn bow or rifle barrel should ever be directed toward another hunter or oneself. Riding or climbing with a loaded gun is only begging for an accident.

Also, a flashlight can save one's life from a less-than-careful hunter. Assuredly, all hunters know that no deer ever carries a flashlight while walking through the woods. Thus, before daybreak while walking to a stand and then again at dusk while walking back, the deer hunter should always carry a flashlight showing a good, bright beam. Many hunters leave their flashlight immediately at the base of the tree that they climb, so it is readily available when they start their trek back to a vehicle or camp. A few leaves ruffled over the metal of the light covers any reflection that might be noticed by deer or other hunters.

Moreover, for safety's sake, a hunter-orange cap or vest is more readily seen by another hunter, and it is a good idea to wear such color whether the law requires it or not. On some hunts, 144 square inches of hunter-orange is required by law.

Falling, gun accidents, exposure to cold, heart attacks from overexertion, becoming lost, and misidentifying one's target constitute many hunting hazards.

Also, in some regions of the country, certain wild animals may be dangerous to the deer hunter, such as black bears, grizzly bears,

Hunter safety is a must. Eddie Evans, a hunting partner of the author's, displays a huge rattler (now headless) that gave the author a close call during an early-season bow hunt.

Hunter boots with nylon safety mesh between the leather provides much-needed safety while in rattler country. However, should the hunter get bitten, an antivenom shot within thirty minutes is critical.

Danger from wild animals depends upon the region in which you hunt. Northern and western hunters may be within the grizzly's range. Hunters in southern swamps and bayous may be within the alligator's home range.

wild boars, alligators, and poisonous snakes. Obviously, whether the deer hunter were in the far North or in southern swamps dictates the danger from specific wild animals. In my region of the Southeast, rattlesnakes are common, and during bow season the hunter should be mindful of them.

I almost stepped on a rattler once while looking upward at treetops for an alternate tree for my stand. Only my peripheral vision and the fact that it was a little cool for September prevented the rattler from striking me. Chaps, leggings, and snakeproof, hightopped boots should be worn while bow hunting the southern swamps in September, October, and into November. Rattlers do come out to sun on rock ledges and try to catch one last chipmunk or squirrel, even into November, throughout much of the South.

Within the United States, the various species of rattlers, the copperhead, the true cottonmouth, and the coral snake are the four types of poisonous snakes. The coral snake lives only in the Deep South, from near Birmingham, Alabama, southward through Florida in sandy soil. Snakes are cold-blooded and cannot tolerate very cold weather; thus, deer hunters in the northern states are relatively free of this danger.

Regardless of where you deer hunt, it is a good idea to separate your food supply, empty cans, and garbage from the sleeping quarters. Raccoons or stray dogs rattling around among empty food cans may upset your sleep. Further, attacks by bears, should they be in the vicinity, often come from the animal's search for a free handout. Thus, it is not only safer but wiser to cache your food, if possible and practical, away from the sleeping quarters, particularly if the hunt is within the grizzly bear's range.

Chapter 3

The White-tailed Deer

An Escape Artist

"They're just looking for something to run from!" said Paul McBride, a fifteen-year veteran deer hunter and friend of mine. That was in the predawn darkness one time as we headed down the trail toward our tree stands. We were whitetail hunting on the Cumberland Plateau near the Tennessee and Alabama border.

After hunting, researching, and studying *Odocoileus virginianus*, the white-tailed deer, I know of no better sentence than Paul's for describing this fascinating and challenging big-game animal. For truly, a whitetail is an escape artist even when the hunter has the deer within his sights. Plus, the whitetail performs his evasive tricks over a relatively small land area when compared to other large game animals. In doing so, the whitetail familiarizes himself with practically every object that he sees. Few strange objects escape his attention, and he spends several minutes looking over and checking out any new form and shape that invades his living quarters.

The whitetail, however, does have certain obvious physical limitations that every serious deer hunter should know about. For exam-

A trophy-racked, whitetailed buck is the most highly sought big-game animal on earth. But a wily old buck, six or seven years old, is an escape artist. Practically no sound, scent, or movement within his domain goes unnoticed. He dominates lesser bucks while he is in his prime. (Drawing by Dixie Holcomb)

ple, in form interpretation the whitetail may do a very poor job — the first time. In other words, the whitetail may not distinguish what the hunter is the first time he sees a camouflaged object up in a tree stand. But you can bet your lunch that, in all likelihood, the whitetail will be much more wary the next time he sees you hanging out there in space up in your tree stand.

The hunter who can remain as motionless as possible upon a whitetail's approach and still wield his gun or bow effectively is well on the way to becoming a successful deer hunter.

Deer obviously do recognize their own silhouette shape, the form of woodland animals, and other woodland objects. But, of course, a deer cannot understand technological objects and what these objects do. Neither, upon first sight, does a deer understand a new object twenty feet up in a tree stand, so many hunters rely on this technique in harvesting the whitetail. Such are some of the characteristics of the wary whitetail. They learn from an initial encounter and certainly retain this memory pattern for at least several days, maybe the remainder of their life. Further, by his nervous, alert demeanor, the same startled deer conveys this message to other deer through its various communicative means.

I have observed separate deer exhibiting a nervous response while passing the exact spot where another deer had been shot at with a bow, startled, and ran. From my tree stand, just at dusk, I had simply shot over the previous deer. Two different deer later came to the exact plot of ground, sniffed around, and showed nervous action and demeanor. The two events were twenty-four hours apart.

A hunting partner of mine, Eddie Evans, declares that he watched a whitetail sniff the exact spot on a sapling he had touched with his hand thirty-six hours earlier.

Even though the whitetail is poor at understanding a new object the first time he encounters it, should the object move, it then becomes an altogether different story. The whitetail has thrived over thousands of years by detecting and responding to movements— namely the movements of predators.

To a whitetail, any movement within woods signals the possibility of danger. Normally, however, a deer can tell the difference between animal and inanimate movement. A whitetail gets good at recognizing the difference between natural woodland movement and associated sounds, and unnatural commotion—like a novice deer hunter clanking up a gnarled hickory tree. Branches, acorns, hickory nuts, and leaves falling to the forest floor are readily recognized by deer. While the rustling sounds made by birds and squirrels are a part of the deer's everyday world, one snapping twig broken by a stalking

Deer do learn that hunters climb and sit in trees. No doubt the whitetail retains this memory after once viewing or hearing the hunter in his stand. For several days, then, the whitetail may alter his trails to evade the stand.

hunter is not a normal sound. Deer intuitively know that only other large animals, predators perhaps, can snap twigs by stepping on them. Thus, the whitetail is constantly on the alert.

The Whitetail's Reactions

Probably the greatest distinguishing deficiency the whitetail has, though, is that of light interpretation at night. Consequently, the spotlighting of deer takes near complete advantage of them as they stand stupefied by the light. Spotlighting, of course, is not in the realm of deer hunting sport and is outlawed as it certainly should be in hunting. Game managers and biologists may use this technique, however, in estimating population density, carrying capacity of the land, and in doing other scientific observations of the deer herd.

A much-debated topic among deer hunters is whether or not a wounded deer runs uphill or downhill while fleeing the hunter. My observation has been that a wounded deer may do either or both, depending on several factors such as terrain, location of the hunter, and proximity to the deer's main escape routes. In general, a white-tail conserves all the energy he can, even in fleeing. Normally, though, after a deer is wounded, he may run uphill a short distance, but he will usually turn downhill and travel along the closest escape route. More important, a wounded deer usually backtracks the way he came.

Over most hilly terrain the whitetail prefers to make his trails between draws and up ravines that have the easiest access for day-in and day-out travel. Thus, over a half-mile mountainside, there will likely be three or four main trails that serve as escape routes. Wounded deer, if given a choice, will often follow one of these.

Most escape routes do lead downhill toward creeks and water. The whitetail seeks these natural watering places in evading the hunter and in slaking his own thirst from loss of blood. A whitetail in the wild state, flaring the white flag that gives him his name, has a natural impulse to run when alerted.

Once while attending a deer seminar on the whitetail, I visited a university's deer research farm. The biologists there had secured a buck deer that had been born blind. The young buck had survived long enough before capture to acquire fully his wild nature. Thus, when one approaches the blind buck's penned quarters, the deer

The flag formed by the deer's tail gives him his name. All too often this is the part of the whitetail seen by the hunter. Other deer, when seeing a member of the herd erect his flag, react to this important woodland signal.

takes off running. The blind buck, however, runs only in about a four-foot circle free of objects — really going nowhere — even though his penned enclosure is much larger than that. The point is, though, that once a whitetail becomes wild, it is extremely difficult for him to ever be tamed.

The natural characteristic of the white-tailed deer is not to run any great distance when startled or wounded, unless he detects the hunter in pursuit. When the hunter wounds a deer, it is a good policy, if practical, to wait two hours or so before trailing. A deer, unless mortally wounded on the spot, will more than likely run two hundred to three hundred yards and stop. Then, if not startled further, that may be as far as the deer goes. Often, the hunter who locates the blood trail then waits about two hours will find his deer within a short distance from where he originally shot it.

Otherwise, should the deer know that someone is following closely, the hunter may have a real chase in trying to keep up with the wounded deer. Many wounded deer are lost this way. So, it is best to locate the wounded deer's direction of flight, find the blood trail, and then later find your harvested whitetail, perhaps close by.

Once on a muzzleloader hunt, a hunting friend of mine wounded a deer and, due to our schedule, we had to trail the whitetail soon afterward. Even though the quarry was severely hit and leaving a heavy blood trail, we jumped the deer within about 200 yards. With an immobilized front quarter, the whitetail still cleared a five-foot ledge and struck for the valley below through thick brush.

As it turned out, after about a half-mile chase through the brambles, another hunter harvested the deer and said that he did not know the deer had been wounded because of its rapid flight. Such episodes are a tribute to the whitetail's toughness as the most evasive of big-game animals.

The whitetail is a highly social animal, and that relates directly to hunter success. After a fawn is about six weeks old, it starts following its mother. By so doing the young deer learns to eat several different kinds of food. It learns to be wild as a survival technique. Also, the fawn learns his mother's home range. At about three months, the fawn does not have to suckle and becomes independent in seeking food.

All members of a deer herd do not live together as one large group. Instead, they form several small subgroups of perhaps four or five deer, and these groups eat and bed near one another. Often, these small subgroups meet other groups at watering holes or feeding areas once or twice a day. These small social groups add to survival possibilities, as the deer disperse into different directions most of the time.

Other whitetail social habits, such as bucks running in bachelor groups, fighting for dominance, and seasonal rutting of both the buck and doe, may cause the deer to be more conspicuous to the hunters. Natural social bonds that hold the deer activities together longer are the doe-fawn relationships during summer and into fall and winter. The older fawn is not really dependent upon the doe, but follows the doe over the same home range that has recently been learned. Hunters should not be overly concerned about harvesting does on either-sex deer hunts after the fawns are food-independent from the does.

Summer bachelor groups of bucks later break up as the larger, better-antlered bucks start making power plays for dominance and breeding of the does. Undoubtedly, the most significant whitetail social relationship that appeals to the hunter is the rut. Specifically, the rut provides the trophy hunter with his greatest opportunity for a large rack because the largest, strongest, and best-racked bucks do most of the breeding and woodland rambling to meet that end.

Furthermore, during the rutting season the bucks can be fooled and lured easier than at any other time because their attention is both distracted by and lured toward sexual activities of the does. Since the buck has been incapable of sexual activities during the spring and summer, the natural urge to breed is intensified during the relatively short rutting season.

Doe urine lures drifting on the wind currents, so placed by the hunter, may draw the bucks within range. Also, the hunter rattling antlers together from a hidden position may draw the larger bucks in. These two efforts by the hunter — the latter mocking two fighting bucks, and the first one using natural secretions from the doe's urinary tract — greatly entice bucks to get in on the actions that supposedly involve other deer. During the rut, then, the buck is more a lover and rambles around by himself. This is unlike the behavior of the doe and her fawns and older does that often walk single file over their trails. This social habit of single-file walking within the woodland can either be a plus or a minus for the hunter.

The hunter can hear the deer coming much quicker and easier because they make more noise. However, while walking together, the deer are more likely to see the hunter should he make much movement.

Chapter 4

Daily Habits of Whitetails

Trail Patterns

When undisturbed by hunters or natural enemies, the white-tailed deer's trail schedule can be quite predictable, and it is the lucky hunter who can figure this out. If unharassed, the deer settles into his seasonal patterns and browses on his choice foods at certain times. The constant challenge to any serious deer hunter then is to find where the deer are browsing and bedding. After locating the deer's main trails, the hunter then either sits on stand over them or stalks those sites where the deer are likely to travel.

In the eastern woodlot, farming, and wilderness sections of the United States, deer hunters, more and more, are using the tree-stand method in deer hunting. The challenge then is to first locate well-used deer trails and, secondly, to climb a tree within easy shot range for a clean harvest with either gun or bow.

The whitetail deer hunter, though, should scout a lot or he may never know the many shifts in pattern that the deer make. Some of these changes may be minor and of short duration. For example, the deer may be making side trips to preferred foods for only a week or

When undisturbed, the whitetail is a creature of habit and often walks the same trails leading to seasonal food sources. In doing so, the deer walk in tandem file and make narrow trails a few inches wide. The hunter who scouts and finds these worn trails may harvest his deer by placing a tree-stand adjacent to the trail. Here, the deer have formed a trail between two sections of woodland in the Smoky Mountains in east Tennessee.

so. Also, it is not likely that a whitetail will walk all of his trails every day. Consequently, deer may walk a certain trail every other day, or every third or fourth day on a more variable schedule. Some hunters go by the policy of watching a trail position for three days in succession before giving up on the spot. Here, only the hunter's total field experience and common sense can tell him when to choose another spot.

As part of their daily habits, deer often move to or from their browsing choices near dawn and dusk. This activity then requires that the hunter be on stand early in the morning and late in the day. A typical deer hunt may begin at three or four o'clock in the morning.

Next, the hunter has the job of getting safely to his preselected tree and climbing it in the dark, using the correct equipment for the hunt. Many predawn and post-sunset activities are involved in trying to fool a white-tailed deer. The hunter must be as quiet as possible while doing all of these activities, or his chances are much reduced in getting his quarry.

Too, as the hunter tries to match his own schedule with the daily habits of the deer, transportation to and from the hunting spot is sometimes a big factor. Tree stand, food, water, clothing, personal items, flashlight, and bow or gun must be safely carried as the hunter attempts to get up in his tree before the break of dawn.

The hunter must do all of this without falling, freezing, getting lost, or worse, injuring himself or some other hunter. Deer hunting is a tough, demanding sport that is full of tall tales, heartbreaks, heroics (after fireside retellings!), long shots, and near misses. Were it not so, deer hunting would not be the popular sport that it is. Now, this growing outdoor sport is enabling more hunters to collect their meat and trophies and enjoy the challenge of their forefathers.

Eating Habits

Much of the whitetail's daily activity that impacts hunter effort stems from the deer's digestive anatomy, food requirements, and subsequent browsing habits. The deer has a four-compartment stomach and fills the front pouch first. This relates directly to the evasion of predators, but it causes the hunter a lot of scouting time. To evade predators, the whitetail browses for an hour or so, then beds while chewing his cud and completing the digestive process. The main survival advantage in this daily habit places the deer out of predator and hunter view for hours at a time. The deer, then, does not have to stand exposed to increased danger while completing the entire digestive process. A whitetail eats for a short time then hides for a longer time. This trick of nature places the deer out of obvious view during many of the daylight hours.

However, deer do eat about every four hours. Dawn and dusk usually find the deer going to or from their browsing spots. The whitetail also browses more at noon than most hunters realize. Since browsing peaks occur every four or five hours, one hits near noon. The deer hunter also becomes hungry at midday. But the hunter who can stay on stand through the lunch hour increases his chances of bagging a deer. Such dedication, then, provides another opportunity for the hunter to bag a wary whitetail.

Since the deer is a browser instead of a grazer, his diet consists of lots of cellulose material from twigs and plant shoots. Even after cud-chewing and digestion, the deer's droppings still contain obvious amounts of undigested, woody, cellulose material. Following browsing on this diet, the fecal droppings from deer are small and pellet-shaped, about one-fourth inch in diameter. Should, however, the deer utilize much green, leafy vegetation, especially in spring and early summer, the fecal droppings are deposited in less discrete packets and form small mounds about one inch high and two or three inches in diameter.

The hunter, though, will soon learn these trail signs while scouting. Droppings, of course, show one sure sign that a deer has been in that exact location. So, the relative number of droppings, deer tracks, browse sign on vegetation tips, bedding imprints, buck rub marks on saplings, hoof marks made in feeding, and buck scrapes all constitute good, positive indications of the whitetail's habits and locations.

Deer generally drink once a day. During the fall much deer activity is centered near permanent watering holes. July, August, and September are usually seasonally dry periods with little rain over much of the United States. Then the mud-puddles, smaller ponds, and creek beds often dry up and force the deer to year-round watering points. In the wilderness, permanent watering points are usually artisian pools that are fed from the underground water table instead

Fecal droppings from deer are usually pellet-shaped. When found upon the forest floor, they are a sure sign that a deer was there. When deer browse on many kinds of shrubs, their fecal droppings contain less water and more fiber, and are in discrete units.

of from surface run-off water. Permanent water holes are especially advantageous to the fall bow hunter. One good way for the bow hunter to zero-in on a possible wilderness pool is to, first, observe a reliable topographical map before scouting. A tree stand located near a drought pool that presents an open shooting lane through camouflaged shrub canopies makes an ideal bow hunting location.

The scouting hunter may often find these small but permanent pools at the head of dry creek beds over the eastern United States. Here, even though permanent, the pools do not flow enough to form a running creek during a drought. Thus, this drought situation concentrates the whitetail trail activity even more, as the deer are forced to these critical watering points that may only be a few feet in diameter. In his topo-map observation, the hunter should look for the beginnings of such creeks. Often these beginning points will be in heavy rock formations in ravines. Close contour lines, usually brown, will show on the map. The permanent pools are usually shown in blue color points on most topo maps.

In reading topo maps, relatively wide distances between contour lines show flats or gentle slopes within the woodland. Over the eastern United States, these woodland benches are often covered with various species of oaks. The white oak tree, especially, bears acorns that are tasty and nutritious to the browsing deer. Hunter observation will show that the deer form part of their main trails through oak flats. There are two good reasons for this: food availability and less energy required in walking.

Acorns make up one of the main mast crops for deer. On some game preserves, acorns provide about 80 percent of the deer's autumn and/or wintertime diet, since these nuts are quite accessible to browsing whitetails. Paw marks and ruffled leaves show where deer have searched for acorns over the forest floor. These paw marks, along with droppings and bedding imprints, are direct proof that deer are using the area.

A tree, then, selectively chosen near the hot spot of the trail, and presenting shooting lanes, gives the hunter a definite advantage after he ascends his tree stand. While walking over trails, deer do look up. And when walking up an inclined trail, the deer's field of vision would include a distance several feet above ground level. For this reason, a tree stand placed immediately at the head of an incline is not the best choice. Here, the deer can likely detect any movement that the hunter makes. In this situation, it is better for the hunter to back off about thirty yards or so and choose a tree that presents a flatter sight trajectory to the deer. Then, when the deer has his head down nibbling on acorns, the hunter can more effectively make his shot toward the deer's vital zone right behind the whitetail's foreleg.

However, at this critical point in hunting, seemingly anything can happen. A sapling can suddenly spring up from nowhere; a gun that has never jammed can jam; an arrow can fall from its rest when the hunter draws his bow; the scope on one's rifle can fog up; the powder in a muzzleloader may have accumulated moisture and not ignite; a bow string may break; worse, a bow limb may break; the hunter may strike his bow against the tree stand; or another hunter may come wandering by at exactly the wrong instant and startle a group of whitetails.

But, whatever the mistake that cost you a deer, you will always remember it over your hunting career—along with the heartbreak and disappointment. Later, however, the experience may become one of your favorite campfire stories. The important thing, of course, is that the hunter learns from his mistakes and tries to keep them to a minimum. Thus, over the years, the outdoorsman becomes a veteran deer hunter.

While up in a tree stand and trying to harvest a deer going about his daily routine, the hunter's greatest challenge is getting the job done before being detected by the whitetail. Clothing rubbed against tree bark, a creaking tree stand, or any metallic, unnatural sound will likely startle the deer. This instant shows the white-tailed deer at his wary best. Deer become experts in recognizing the difference between natural and unnatural sounds, and in order to do this, they must constantly search and listen.

Season and Weather Patterns

Early in the hunting season, before the whitetail's daily patterns have been upset by hunters, is the most predictable time to harvest a deer. If the hunter makes it up into his tree stand without affecting the area with his human odor, handles the deer's approach correctly, places his shot well, then he likely has his deer.

Late-season deer hunting renders a supreme challenge to many hunters because of the physical demands that it makes. Days that could have been spent in actual hunting now must be spent in scouting. The fall droughts are gone, and the deer are no longer concentrated around isolated, permanent water holes. Instead, both the hunter's transportation roads and smaller woodland trails are pockmarked with countless freezing and thawing puddles that make accessibility more difficult.

In mountainous regions, hunter accessibility can become next to impossible without a reliable 4WD vehicle backed up with a front-end winch. For, often in freezing rain or snow, the deer hunter goes to great inconvenience and effort to find the whitetail in its greatly altered wintertime daily patterns.

Such late-season, wintertime hunting is the great eliminator of many less-hearted, less-dedicated, or ill-equipped deer hunters. Rationally, however, temperatures may drop to a point at which wintertime deer hunting is dangerous, even to the most hardy and best-equipped hunters. Chill factors, depending upon the latitude and altitude, can plummet to intolerable conditions.

Still . . . that big buck, maybe a Boone and Crockett record, is out there somewhere. And daily life still goes on in the deer family. But winter deer kills from the deep, packed snow and subzero temperatures take their toll on the population. Many die of starvation and by freezing. In many northern states, winter kill often numbers into the thousands. The winter pattern for the whitetail is to yard up and simply try to last out the deathly cold weather by utilizing the last bit of stored fat that was packed on in the fall. Any hunter must then find the deer's yarding areas. Trail activity is at a bare minimum, as the deer move very little in their daily habits.

Other less drastic weather conditions affect the whitetail's daily patterns. For instance, deer browse and move over their woodland trails during light, gentle rains, but during drenching downpours they seek cover. After a rain, when the woodland leaves are moist and pliable, is a good time to stalk-hunt as opposed to tree-stand hunting. Then, slowly making your way through the forest, stopping and searching for standing or bedded deer, the stalk hunter may take his prey. Leaves and forest twigs, of course, are not as likely to break and crackle underfoot. On the other hand, deer may very well escape the hunter's ears, too. The tree-stand hunter is at a similar disadvantage as is the deer, which may pass by undetected at a few yards.

A freeze or frost following a rain, however, hardens the forest-floor vegetation and will once again produce the characteristic crunch-and-rattle sounds when stepped upon. On a frosty morning, then, the deer may be heard coming through the forest woodland until a midday thaw.

Lunar changes—the four phases of the moon—affect the deer's activities, too. But, the ways in which this happens are not well understood. It is known by biologists, however, that the moon and sun exert gravitational attractions upon the earth, the oceans, and perhaps on all living plants and animals on earth. Since the two half-moon phases make up fourteen days, or one-half of the total lunar month, deer naturally need to feed within each of these seven-day periods. And their feeding activity seems to be greater then. Moreover, the two half-moon phases are in between the two extremes and represent the average lunar influence from the new moon's darkness and the full moon's brightness.

Also, the two half-moon phases represent an average of the gravitational attractions, too. Many natural cycles, including the onset of the doe's sexual heat cycle, is based on a twenty-eight-day lunar

The whitetail moves over a wintertime home range that is about one-tenth the size of their summer home range. In extremely cold weather and deep snow, the deer simply yard up and try to survive the winter by using the last bit of their stored fat.

month. It stands to reason, then, that the doe's sexual activities are influenced by lunar phases. Then indirectly, during the rut, the buck is affected also, if for no other reason than the influence of the doe's sexual activity.

Any observant hunter can tell that a whitetail has a large set of eyes for it's body size. That means, of course, that the surface area is relatively large on the retina of the deer's eye. Further, biologists know that the cells on the deer's retina are largely rods which function in near-darkness and are good at detecting movement but not color. For this reason the whitetail feeds and is active at night during the new-moon phase when little light is reflected from the moon. Then, at least from man, one predator down through the ages, the deer has been free.

Some hunters also believe that when the peak of the rut matches the dark-of-the-moon, or new moon, phase, deer are more active. This may be true, unless the deer are influenced by other natural variables. Here, even though all the physical and biological mechanisms are not understood and are complex, it is reasonable to assume that the amount of light and gravitational attraction in relation to the earth's latitude and temperatures bear upon the whitetail's physiology and daily activity patterns.

In summary, then, many hunters have found that deer are more active in their daily patterns during the new-moon and half-moon phases, but are less active during the seven-day full-moon period.

Chapter 5

Survival Tactics
of Whitetails

Physical Capabilities

The white-tailed deer is well adapted to live and survive close to man. During the course of animal evolution, the whitetail has evolved external and internal capabilities that promote his techniques in evading predators.

The deer's first source for survival is his nose. It has been said with much truth that the whitetail lives or dies by his nose. A young fawn learns the nature of evasion after living only a few days with its mother. Any new smell sensed by a deer over its home range is treated with suspicion. Deer soon learn that the hunter represents danger and is cautiously avoided.

Deer course slowly over their home range. Their nature is to walk only a few feet, then stop and test the air currents with their noses. By using this technique, the whitetail remains inconspicuous within the forest because his movements are slow and deliberate.

Also, relative to man, deer have much larger eyes, which are equipped for better night vision than man's. Too, deer have excellent peripheral vision due to the location of their eyes in the head.

In the eye systems of higher animals, there are two main types of cells: rod cells and cone cells. Rod cells are for night vision and movement detection. Cone cells are for color perception. Whereas man is well equipped with cone cells for color perception, the white-tailed deer is better equipped with rod cells for night vision and detecting movement.

This difference in visual capability often comes into play just at dark for the deer hunter in his tree stand. Legal and safe shooting time for the hunter, of course, ends at dusk. Consequently, the last fifteen minutes or so of daylight may be the most profitable time for the hunter to harvest his deer. Quite often the arrival of nightfall calls for the hunter's best discipline and techniques. Just before dark, deer start moving over their trails. The bow hunter must then make slow, deliberate movements from his tree-stand perch. The muzzleloader hunter may best switch hands and shoot wrong-handed rather than risk total body movement, should the deer walk up on the wrong shooting side of him. And for the high-powered rifle hunter, an illuminator scope gives partial advantage back to the hunter as the last light rays are gathered by the scope for better sighting.

Even though the white-tailed deer is an expert at smelling and detecting movement, he is not good at interpreting the functions of object shapes. For example, it is not unusual for deer to detect a hunter in his tree stand. But, just because the whitetail sees the hunter, it does not mean that the deer understands what the hunter is. So the rule of thumb is to remain quiet and motionless when the deer approaches. Often the whitetail is convinced that you are just another forest object and passes on by you.

Therefore, with an excitedly pounding pulse as he draws his bow or aims his rifle, the hunter must appear motionless to the deer. In this particular instant, in this drama of life and death, it is amazing how the whitetail often manages to survive. Any sound, any movement, or any unseen sapling hit by the hunter can send the whitetail on his tail-flaring way and foil a shot.

Many have been bow hunters who, even at full-draw and with the deer only yards ahead, have made some nearly inaudible noise or made some slight movement and startled this wary animal. Thus, rubberized bow and gun holders on your tree stand are a must to help deaden sound. Whitetails have an uncanny ability to distin-

Deer soon learn to recognize sounds, both threatening and non threatening, such as those made by this bird. Birds, squirrels, and chipmunks scratch and rattle a lot among the leaves. These natural sounds are ignored by the wary whitetail. Metallic sounds or twig-crackling sounds, however, alert the deer. The hunter, while walking through the woods or near his stand, should be as quiet as possible.

guish between natural sounds, nonthreatening sounds, and any man-made sounds. While ambling over their woodland trails, deer constantly interpret many sounds: falling timber; scurrying squirrels; birds scratching among dry leaves; falling acorns and hickory nuts; leaves blown by the wind rattling against tree bark; airplanes flying low overhead; farm machinery rumbling over a nearby field; plus many other nonthreatening sounds. But, in woodland situations and context, none of these sounds will startle the wary whitetail as quickly as one dry twig crackled by a hunter's foot or one slight squeak cause by an arrow shaft drawn across an arrow rest by the bow hunter.

Camouflaging and Demeanor

When startled, though, deer do not run out of their home range. Usually, when startled or wounded, the whitetail doubles back upon his own trail, heading in the direction from which he came. A deer knows that it should be a safe route because of his recent familiarity with it.

Moreover, a deer's body has evolved a natural camouflaging system. The whitetail bears the natural dark color on its back and the light color on its stomach. In winter when the whitetail is viewed by the hunter from an elevated position, its body is quite inconspicuous and hard to see against the dark forest floor and gray-barked trees. Also, were a predator or a hunter looking uphill at a whitetail highlighted against the brightness of the sky, the deer's white stomach blends in with the background.

Deer begin their lives camouflaged. As dappled, spotted fawns, they merge with the light and dark shadows over the forest floor. Too, until a month or so old, fawns move little and stay where the doe places them. As a survival tactic, this seclusive nature is important to the young deer. Wildlife scientists believe that the young fawn's nervous system is so constructed that the youngster cannot move when greatly frightened. This is a definite survival advantage for the fawn when it is only a few days old. For, should it try to run at this young age, it is highly unlikely that the young deer could evade any large predator. So, on the average and over the long run, it is better that the fawn stay put and hopefully go undetected.

As whitetails mature—both bucks and does—they camouflage

Deer are naturally camouflaged to the hunter's eye. Their coats blend with the tree trunks, light and shadows, and fallen debris over the forest floor. Further, the buck's antlers, legs, and general body form are not easily recognized among the saplings, trees, and shrubs in his surroundings.

from the hunter's sight in several other ways. Even though deer may weigh around 200 pounds or more when grown, their legs, neck, and antlers (for bucks) camouflage well in size and shape with saplings, shrubs, and small trees. In the wintertime when food is scarce, it is characteristic of whitetails to conserve energy in their daily routine. Consequently, deer stand idle a lot in the woodland. Here, standing still among trees and saplings, they are naturally camouflaged to the casual observer. Further, when the deer does walk, he does so in a stealthy manner, going slowly, and still blending with his surroundings. It is for these reasons that deer appear, seemingly, from nowhere as phantoms to the hunter. The whitetail can be within a few yards of the hunter, and neither may know it. Also, should the deer be the first to discover it, he may wait-out the hunter, sensing somehow that the hunter is unaware of the animal's presence. The stalk-hunter then does well to duplicate this slow, deliberate pace of the deer. After practicing this slow-motion type of walking, the hunter, too, soon learns its benefit as a stalking technique. The hunter, with practice, will sense the slow rhythm required for stalk-hunting as he moves over the terrain.

In developing this slow rhythm, the hunter covers less ground. But every five yards or so he brings new terrain features into view, and a big buck could be hiding or bedding just over a ridge or in a draw. For the bow hunter this stalking technique is probably his greatest challenge, with much less chance of success than with a firearm. The bow hunter who can do it, though, has accomplished a feat worthy of a campfire recount.

Stalk-hunting with a .30-06, 3X9-power scoped rifle, for instance, is considerably more effective, of course, although perhaps not as challenging. Some deer hunters prefer this method to using a tree stand, and become proficient at stalk-hunting. The stalk-hunter will quickly learn that, as opposed to tree-stand hunting, less layered clothing is required, as production of body heat is much greater.

No deer hunter has to be told about the running and jumping abilities of his quarry. Clearing a six-foot fence is no big challenge for a large buck. Broad-jumping a twenty-foot ditch and leaving the hunter 300 yards behind is no task either, since at top speed the deer can reach thirty miles per hour. But, even under heavy hunting pressure, deer generally do not leave their home range; they just become more expert at utilizing it to their advantage.

Thus, within their relatively small home-range area, the whitetail memorizes the ravines, thickets, swamps, timber stands, woodland benches, meadows, break areas, watering holes, seasonal browsing places, and most of all, the various escape routes from each. Then, as hunting pressure increases, the whitetail further changes his daytime and nighttime routines. Toward the end of the hunting season, even the most ardent and experienced hunters are presented a variety of greatly changed patterns.

Late in the hunting season, the easily recognized, repetitive patterns that occurred in the early bow season are gone. In short, the whitetail figures out the hunter's habits, too. For instance, should the hunter muff a shot and the deer see him during their evening run, the deer will change their trail pattern to a different time of day, or avoid that particular spot altogether for a while. For the hunter, then, alternate hunting areas are always important as the season progresses.

As a survival tactic, whitetails piece together the sights, sounds, and scents made by hunters, and alter patterns accordingly over the hunting season. Also, in moving over their trails, deer often walk in line, following one another. By so doing, they pay great attention to the deer in front of them. Tail flicking is a major means of communication among deer while on trail. The casual side-to-side tail flick, which alternately shows their white rump and short, brown tail, signals that there is no danger ahead in the immediate area. As most deer browse and slowly walk over their trails, they display this message to any deer that may be behind.

When alerted, though, the deer lifts his tail erect. Should danger be close at hand, the deer flares the entire tail over its rump area and displays its much-flared white, rear quarters. This is the familiar sight often seen by the unlucky hunter as the deer bounds safely into the forest. This tail-flaring characteristic is what gave this species its common name.

Digestive Adaptation

Not only outwardly and physically have white-tailed deer evolved survival tactics, but inwardly and physiologically they have as well. For living in the wild, deer are physiologically adapted in their digestive organs to browse upon a multitude of food sources. Deer naturally like some of these better than others. Berries, acorns, and other fruits such as apples are choice selections, and some hunters use these scents while hunting to both cover their own scent and to attract deer.

The hunter trying to discover the deer's trail patterns must take these food-production areas into account. Some vegetative sources such as wild berries may be available for only two or three weeks while others such as white oak acorns last for a few months. Deer, when pressured by increased hunter activity, will choose alternate browsing sites, and similarly, the hunter must seek out alternate hunting areas. The fine-tuning of the hunter's scouting techniques are crucial in this situation. Time spent in the same tree stand after deer have obviously shifted patterns is only wasted time that could be better spent in scouting and trying to piece together new feeding patterns.

Moreover, to escape predators, deer browse and shortly move to their bedding sites to regurgitate, chew their cud, and digest their food through their four-segmented stomach. While doing this, the deer bed with their noses into the prevailing air currents to sense any predators on the prowl. This specialized habit keeps the deer out of view of would-be predators. Over evolutionary time, then, the whitetail's short browsing periods, followed by bedding in secluded areas, permits the deer better overall chances for survival.

The hunter's scouting shows where the whitetails choose cane-brakes, cedar stands, and weed thickets as prime bedding places. In winter especially, these areas are chosen by the deer for protection from both predators and cold temperatures.

Even when hit by the hunter, the whitetail still demonstrates his strong survival capabilities. For instance, when arrowed in a spot where it can be reached, a whitetail, while running at nearly full speed, may grab the arrow by its point and pull the fletched projectile on through. Too, deer will lick and salivate wounds, if possible, to supposedly aid in blood coagulation.

Many hunters have observed that whitetails run downhill when wounded, seek water sources, and finally stand their ground when cornered. Consequently, a wounded buck with antlers, whether lying or standing, should be approached with caution. The buck's evasive actions can suddenly turn to aggression when he is cornered.

Even though evasive in nature, a buck may turn aggressive when cornered or wounded. The hunter then should approach a downed buck with caution. The buck's antlers are lethal weapons when wielded in aggression toward a hunter.

Reproductive Capability

In reproductive capability, the whitetail is made to multiply, too. A healthy doe on good browse usually bears twins. But, under extreme starvation, she may reabsorb her fetus to ensure her own survival. The number of fawns at birth, then, averages near one and a half for fertile does in most herds. Further, on good browse, fawns born early may grow quickly their first year and be bred their first winter.

In surviving winter in the northern states, or at higher altitudes where snow is commonly deep, deer often yard up and try to wait out the cold temperatures in a metabolic state of much-reduced activity. The whitetail's heart rate lowers along with its other biological and physical activities. Wildlife biologists have found that a bedded deer burns 60 percent less energy than it does when standing. Thus, as a final survival tactic under wintertime starvation conditions, a whitetail goes into a lowered energy state that is not unlike hibernation in concept. While doing this, the deer is sustained by the last bit of body fat stored along its backbone.

Luckily, late-summer and early-fall browse permits most whitetail herds to pack on reserve fat along their spines. This reserve energy source usually allows the deer to survive the final cold blasts of winter that precede the spring green-up.

The whitetail is a prolific breeder, and if left to its own devices, it will tend to overpopulate. Thus, enter now the hunter. Under good game management policies, it is better for the herd to be kept below the carrying capacity of its home range.

Finally, then, the hunter winds up as the deer herd's best friend. In short, overall herd survival is enhanced by harvesting individual deer. In the long run this natural arrangement of the predatorial hunter versus the prey deer is mutual. And, when the hunter plays the role of predator, it is soon learned that nature has given the whitetail ample survival abilities to perpetuate his kind. Neither the meat hunter nor the trophy hunter easily fool such a wary animal. If presented a suitable habitat and any kind of sporting chance, the whitetail is made to survive.

Chapter 6

How Antlers Grow

Hormonally Tuned with Nature

Men down through the ages have been fascinated by deer antlers. And it goes without saying that the fascination still remains, especially in meeting the challenge of trophy hunting.

Orientals, for eons, have sought fast-growing animal organs for both therapy and love potions. Their use of deer antlers is no exception. Antlers are the fastest-growing, most proliferating animal organ known. Modern-day scientists are studying the fast but healthy growth of the buck's antlers in hopes of learning why nonhealthy cells caused by cancer grow fast.

Hunters soon learn that antlers and horns are different. Whereas horns on cattle are made of tough protein material like the animal's hoof, antlers on deer are formed from mineral deposits similar to the bony skeleton and skull where the antlers grow attached at the pedicel area.

Usually only bucks have antlers because the male hormone testosterone helps initiate their growth. Nevertheless, should a doe be given injections of the testosterone, she too may grow antlers. A doe in the wild sometimes produces testosterone in her body and thus grows a small set of antlers. So, it is possible that the hunter, sometime during his hunting life, may come across an antlered doe.

Antler growth begins in spring and rapidly accelerates during the summer. During July, for example, the buck may add several inches to the height of his rack. By September the growth is about completed, and the racks become solidified under their velvet cover.

Antler growth is hormonally activated in the spring by day length. Wildlife scientists refer to this definite daylight period as the photoperiod. Bucks that live near the equator, where day length is always twelve hours, begin antler growth at random during the year. But, as one moves farther away from the equator, the seasonal daylight hours change with the degree of latitude in moving from south to north. Consequently, near eighteen degrees latitude, a line-equivalent running near Mexico City, hours of daylight reach about twelve and a half hours in duration.

This amount of light then admitted through the buck's eyes causes hormonal activity first at the base of the buck's brain in the pineal gland. Hormones are activated there which in turn initiate testosterone production in the buck's testes. This male hormone then quickly causes antler production on the buck's skull at the pedicel, and button antlers begin to grow. Growth is slow at first, but it accelerates quickly over the summer.

While the antlers are in the fast-growth phase, much calcium is dissolved from the buck's skeleton, especially from his rib cage, in order to form his rack. It is for this reason that bucks do not produce their biggest racks until they reach full skeletal growth and body weight. The best trophy racks then are usually produced on bucks after they are five and a half to seven and a half years old.

Dietary factors come into play, too. Calcium, phosphorus, and proteins are necessary for best rack production. The buck's diet then can alter the best antler production, regardless of his age.

The male hormone testosterone reaches its maximum production just prior to the onset of the rut and sperm production. Thus, full-hardening of the mineral contents and maximum rack size are well timed with the buck's breeding activity. Moreover, the best-racked bucks are usually the dominant ones within the herd, and they do more of the breeding. The end result is that the best and healthiest

Testosterone, a male hormone, is produced in a buck's testes. The testes shown here were taken from a field-dressed buck. Testosterone production figures heavily into a buck's rack growth, dominance, aggressiveness, and antler casting. This intricate hormonal production is started by the length of daylight, known as the photoperiod. Upon harvesting a buck, removal of the male organs is the first step in field dressing. Recent research has shown that the sperm from a trophy buck may be collected at this time, frozen, and used later for artificial insemination of does.

bucks pass on more genetic material and better survival potential to future deer generations.

So the answer to the question, "Why do bucks grow antlers?", is "To help perpetuate a healthy and well-adapted deer herd." We can see then that a well-racked, dominant buck exhibiting his own strong sexual desires is necessary for the well-being of the future white-tailed deer population.

Furthermore, the game manager who controls his herds by allowing the correct amount of hunting pressure in conjunction with food and habitat availability for the population also enhances its health.

Over time, then, man's quest for the wary whitetail benefits both parties: the hunter and the hunted, the predator and the prey.

The peak of the rut over most of the United States occurs between November and January. Following the rut, the testosterone production in the buck's testes greatly decreases, and the buck goes through a drastic physiological, hormonal, and demeanor change. He becomes more docile and much less aggressive toward other deer.

The antlers begin to disintegrate at their bases and by February or March, over most latitudes, the bucks have cast their racks. The pedicel area of the buck's skull then heals, and this annual process is completed. But, within a few weeks, the antler buttons begin to form again, and the buck goes through a similar hormonal, physiological, behavioral, and sexual experience the next season.

The white-tailed deer expresses his best adaptive traits in the temperate, cold climates. Proof of this is shown by the number of Boone and Crockett and Pope and Young record racks taken from states that have cold winters.

Evolution of Antlers

There are good biological and scientific principles that support why more record racks are found in cold climates. First, Bergmann's Rule, a biological principle, states that, generally, the largest members of any warm-blooded animal species will be found in the most northern parts of its range. The reason? Because more body volume is needed for the animal to survive the cold winters. Consequently, since body size and rack size for deer are generally correlated, the biggest racks then are usually found in the more northern parts of the whitetail's range. A check of the record books shows that states of the Upper Midwest have produced more record racks than those farther south with warmer winters.

Within the last twenty-years, however, whitetail genetic stock has been moved to some of the southern states for breeding purposes. Luckily for the southern hunters, then, more trophy racks are now being produced in the southern reaches of the whitetail's range.

As suspected, though, transportation of this whitetail breeding stock to the South has prompted differentials in timing of rack growth and rutting. As a result the rutting periods are not as exact in the southern states as they are in northern states.

It is becoming more obvious to both wildlife scientists and trophy hunters that it takes a combination of natural factors to produce record racks. Specifically, it takes good herd genetics, proper diet, terrain favorable to the whitetail's living habits and energy conservation, and controlled hunting pressure that allows bucks to mature to about their seventh year.

Many of these combinations match up best in the northern Midwest, the breadbasket of the country. Here, good genetic stock has been passed along. Furthermore, with his agility to live subtly close to man, the whitetail is able to survive within the woodlots, farm-

Well-racked bucks represent a combination of natural factors: age, good genetics, nutritious browse, the buck's energy conservation in extreme cold, suitable terrain, and natural selection over evolutionary time. The largest bucks are usually found in the northern parts of the whitetail's range.

lands, and fencerows that cover much of the Upper Midwest. A rather sparse human population in this farm region coupled with the high-protein content from agricultural crops and natural vegetation sets the stage for continued production of record racks.

River-bottom lands, especially, that provide cover, access to bean, pea, and corn fields — all high-protein foods — are excellent areas for trophy racks. A recent (1982) nontypical set of racks that is a candidate for Boone and Crockett listing was produced near St. Louis, Missouri. This area is near river-bottom land where energy demands are less on bucks than in rough, mountainous terrain.

In mountainous terrain, bucks fighting, maintaining their dominant status, and breeding during the rut are selected more for agility and stamina than for size. Operating, thus, over eons of time by natural selection, the larger bucks have been selected more for flat terrain. Here, body weight is more of a selective breeding advantage than are the agility and stamina needed more in rough, rocky terrain.

Energy flow from calcium- and phosphorus-rich soil through the body of bucks bearing the genetics for good antlers are the requirements for future record racks. Trophy hunters who have lifetime aspirations for taking record-sized racks would do well in concentrating their hunting time in these high-potential areas. In doing so, the trophy hunter is playing the percentages and hunting where the bigger-racked bucks *should* be. Time spent in studying the location of past Boone and Crockett and Pope and Young records is beneficial.

Good herd genetics flow through time with a certain consistency. In other words, those regions and deer herds that have historically produced good racks will continue to do so, provided other natural and predatorial factors, including hunting pressure, remain about the same. For that reason, the Midwest, including the Mississippi River Delta, the Missouri River, the Ohio River, and the Great Lakes regions, and those states bordering middle to eastern Canada should remain the prime producers of whitetail records.

This concept does imply, somewhat, the management of trophy racks and, ultimately, the concepts of hunting sport and fair chase. In short, a whitetail's wild behavior can be modified. Deer can become more docile and easier to harvest. In doing this, though, the great traditional sport of deer hunting would be degraded. Consequently, fair chase in the acquisition of one's quarry becomes paramount. Here, hunters may divide according to their own philosophy of hunting sport. The definition of what constitutes an enclosed area versus a wild, natural condition for whitetails can also become a valid point for debate.

Hunters and biologists alike have learned a lot about deer antlers over the last two centuries. But before the age of scientific observation, the French writer Buffon, in 1756, surmised that a buck's antlers were composed of wood. To save face for the French, however, Cuvier showed that antlers were made from bone in 1817. In retrospect, as erroneous and comical as Buffon's assumption was, he was correct in comparing antler growth patterns with woody plant branches.

A buck typically exhibits monopodial branching in his rack formation. That is, he usually grows a longer, lower antler prong from each side of his skull, and shorter tines project upward from it. Unlike a tree, though, the buck grows and sheds his branched headgear each year as his hormonal system responds to the increase in day length in temperate climates.

Deer antlers may be segregated into two groups: typical and nontypical. A typical set of antlers are usually symmetrically produced on the buck's pedicel areas on the top of his skull. However, like his adversary, the deer hunter, the buck lives in a fallible world, and things and events don't always work right. Consequently, antlers may grow erratically on the buck's skull.

Wildlife scientists have demonstrated through experiments that antlers on white-tailed deer can be made to grow on other parts of the body. For instance, Dr. Richard J. Goss, dean of Biological Sciences at Brown University, successfully demonstrated that antlers can be transplanted and grafted onto a buck's ear. Other animal scientists have, in transplantation experiments, shown that antlers can be induced to grow on a roe buck's foreleg. Such erratically placed racks can grow similarly the next year by an internal biological process called trophical memory. In other words, once started, rack production, shape, and timing tend to occur in the same fashion each year, luckily for the trophy hunter.

At the equator, where day length remains constant each day and lengthening hours of daylight are not an initiating factor, rack production occurs randomly at any time of year. Once antler growth starts, however, the equatorial bucks also settle into an annual, predictable cycle of rack production, with subsequent casting that occurs near the same time annually.

Wildlife biologists have shown the strong possibility that a transition zone exists between ten and seventeen degrees latitude in temperate climates, causing seasonal antler initiation in white-tailed bucks. Closer to the equator than the transitional zone, bucks start their antler growth aseasonally.

Although wildlife scientists have demonstrated under laboratory conditions that antlers may be experimentally grown in bizarre positions on a buck's body, most antlers grow only from the two pedicel areas on top of his skull.

Deer live in a rough-and-tumble world where natural forces, injuries, hardships, and hunger are common occurrences. However, the earth's geophysical forces, leg amputations, hormone imbalances, malnutrition, old age, genetics, and especially injury or any general bruises to a buck fawn's skull are the main causes for erratic rack production. The most critical time for injuries, of course, is prior to the young buck's growing his first set of antlers. Then, once started, the same pattern generally continues through that particular buck's life.

Bruising of the young buck's skull stimulates the buck's nervous system before it does his hormonal system, causing malformed antlers.

Through fables and myths down through the ages, man has told stories about the legendary, one-pronged unicorn. And, as in many myths, there is usually some kernel of truth attached to the folk story. Consequently, through hundreds of thousands of years, men and deer have intermingled over the course of their evolution, the course of the hunting chase, and their day-to-day existence. Thus, many a deer hunter has wondered at the oddly shaped antlers on the head of a white-tailed deer. From nature's standpoint, a deer with an antler growing anywhere on its skull would not have been that unusual in the course of biological and statistical events. To the individual hunter, however, one-time sightings of erratic racks are most impressive.

Mechanical injury is not the only cause of erratic rack growth on a buck; a hormonal dysfunction, similarly, causes nontypical racks to be formed. In jest it could be said that a buck is a hormonal

During summer the buck's tender antlers are covered with velvet. Blood carrying dissolved minerals and food course through the buck's growing rack. This particular buck, still in velvet, shows how well his growing rack camouflages within his natural environment.

animal from one end to the other. Light striking the buck's eyes stimulates the pineal gland at the base of the brain and triggers an elaborate network of hormone production. Finally, other hormones cause testosterone formation in the buck's testes. Testosterone, in varying quantities, acts both as an accelerator or as a braking mechanism on the buck's antler growth, velvet shedding, and rutting behavior. For example, a young castrated buck will grow a set of antlers, but the rack will stay in velvet without shedding. To the late-season hunter, this certainly appears odd.

Testosterone is produced mainly in the testes, with some possible formation in the adrenal glands near the kidneys. This important hormone is produced prolifically during the late fall and early win-

As a final stage in antler development, the bucks rub their dead velvet loose on woodland saplings and small trees. Here, a scouting hunter checks a buck rub on a larger-than-usual tree. In all probability, this rub was made by a well-racked buck. While scouting, the hunter should constantly look for these rub marks.

ter, peaking at the height of the rut. Immediately following the rut, the buck's testosterone level falls dramatically to its lowest annual level. Then, the antler bases dissolve and are shed, but the next year's set of antlers is stimulated to begin. So, the relative lack of testosterone in late winter and early spring initiates antler formation in bucks; but, buildup of the hormone increases rutting activity after the antlers harden, stop growing, and lose their velvet.

Male hormones are called androgens and female hormones are known as estrogens. Thus, both bucks and does produce varying amounts of these body-function regulators according to their sex.

Testosterone, an androgen, may be overly produced in nature by a doe, in which case she may grow a small set of antlers.

Any post-season scouting by the hunter that shows a trophy rack cast within the wilderness should certainly be remembered. For unless some misfortune strikes the buck, in all probability, he will be there next season walking his home-range trails.

Chapter 7

Battling Bucks

Dominance in Whitetail Social Order

Setting man's customary social niceties aside, it must be admitted that the animal world revolves around the quest for power, food, and sex. All three of these endeavors cause a hierarchy in which individual members have their status positions of dominance.

These biological principles are nowhere shown any better than in a deer herd. The constant quest for food, especially during starvation times, coupled with the annual rut, forces members of any deer herd into their individual dominant positions.

Aggression and fighting among animals evolved along with their physical structure. So, when encountered by an opponent, an animal chooses one of three options: fight, flee, or compromise.

Physiologically, a buck's body goes into high gear as the annual rutting season approaches, causing an increase in his aggressive behavior. Researchers in southwest Virginia recently found, after measuring and weighing the testicles of sixty bucks, that during June and July the testes increased in size and weight, producing and storing sperm for the rut that begins in November. Sperm count also

With bulging neck muscles supporting a huge rack, bucks fight for dominance and subsequent breeding of does. This effort permits the healthiest and best-adapted bucks to do most of the breeding. Thus, over time, deer survival is enhanced by the dominant effort of the battling bucks. (Drawing by Dixie Holcomb)

increases with the age of bucks, reaching a plateau at four years of age and declining in older bucks.

Other biologists report that size, weight, age, health, and condition of antlers all help a buck establish his dominance during the actual fighting that occurs primarily during rutting season. And it has been established that yearling bucks and extremely aged ones possess inferior dominance status as compared to five- to six-year-old bucks. As is the usual case with animals, physically, early youth and old age take a back seat to the vigorous exploits of the healthy, young adult in the prime of life. All this, however, serves a purpose in nature's scheme in perpetuation of the species.

With a six-year-old buck coming off summer browse, possessing stored fat, the male hormone level rising toward its annual peak, and a new set of hardened, polished antlers adorning his head, a dominant buck is, literally, the ruler of his woodland domain.

And, that huge, weighty rack which started in velvet several months earlier helped to harden and expand the bulging neck muscles, as the buck whipped and thrashed shrubs and bushes, signaling other bucks to stay off his turf or they'll get the same dose of medicine.

Of course, not all competitors forsake their sexual intentions just because some other buck whipped the bushes over a mountainside. They are going to make him prove that he is tough, and that is when the battles begin. Hence, the bark-denuded bushes are traded for actual head-to-head battle, with the winners exercising power and authority over other challengers.

To the victor go the spoils, and to the winner of many a whitetail fracas go the does during the rut. Thus, the sexual drive, good health, and fighting spirit of the dominant bucks assure the continuation of the species.

Often during the rut, such mundane affairs as eating, sleeping, and caution are tossed to the wind as the buck starts his rambling routes checking his scrapes over his home range.

The easygoing activities and acceptances of the summer social order of the herd fragments during the late fall and winter. Then, it is every buck for himself, as each one internally feels the power of his own body, sensing that he is the man of the hour until shown differently by a more powerful competitor in an antlered, pushing contest.

Initiated earlier by day-length, the male hormone activating agent, the bucks shed their antlers in late winter when the hormonal level changes drastically. Then suddenly, the powerful bucks are without their capable, gouging antlers, and assume a more friendly disposition and filter into a different social order. Some wildlife biologists have found that during the spring and early summer bucks may actually be subordinate to a dominant doe.

Sexual Stimulation

Deer, like other animals of higher order, are creatures of the five senses as they communicate with one another and react to their environment. Furthermore, in the five senses, form and shape recognition play an important part in a deer's life. For example, during the velvet stage in the summer, bucks start recognizing and reacting to dominance as they observe the rack size of other bucks. At this time very few hostile confrontations take place, but each buck becomes increasingly aware of his competitor's rack.

Also, sexually, the buck is stimulated by the physical form of his female counterpart. As simple as the issue may seem on the surface, sexual stimulation among animals is often started by their form and shape perception. Thus, in the case of deer, the sight and smell receptors are greatly relied upon during the rut, when the buck's nostrils become highly tuned to the estrous cycle in does. Then, seeing or smelling a doe causes the sexual arousal that the buck is so physiologically prepared for during the rut.

Some commercial manufacturers now sell form and shape silhouettes of does. These two-dimensional decoys are placed around a tree base and show the hindquarters of a doe. Thus, at least upon first sight, the rutting buck is enticed to investigate this shape silhouette. This doe decoy in conjunction with doe-in-heat lure does have a scientific basis, and the buck, driven by his biological, sexual intentions may well investigate near the hunter's stand.

In the end, the seasonal sexual drive of the buck assures the dropping of fawns in summer, when forbs, browse, and lush vegetation are at their optimum, showing once again how well deer are adapted for survival.

In the evolution of smelling ability, deer are more highly evolved than man. Deer hunters, then, must reckon with their own scent

Sexual stimulation of animals is often enhanced by their sight and scent perceptors. Thus, when a buck sees or smells a doe in sexual heat, he is further stimulated to breed. In this drawing, a sexual lure, a doe's back quarters, is tied to the hunter's tree base. (Drawing by Dixie Holcomb)

when in the deer's vicinity. The deer's ability to smell the hunter's scent, riding on the wind currents, has added to its survival over time.

Survival in the animal kingdom, as in all forms of life, depends upon the primeval success of sex consummation. That means, of course, the male's sperm cell must be deposited close to the female's egg cell, enabling fertilization to occur.

Prior to the actual moment of fertilization, however, physical and geographical barriers must be overcome; so, bounding over many a frost-covered hillside, sniffing the wind currents, bucks have pursued does from time immemorial.

Recently, biologists found that does during estrus produce sexual substances called pheromones which ride on the breeze. Chemically, pheromones are thought to be composed mainly of steroids and fatty acids. Researchers initially discovered pheromones in insects. For example, a male moth can detect a female moth half a mile away by the odoriferous pheromones exuded from her body and dispersed into the air.

The same natural locator and sex-arousal mechanism operates in the deer family, permitting the bucks to detect the sexual status of does during the rut. Consequently, these sexual "perfumes" wafting in the breeze from a frisky doe get the dominant bucks revved into a passionate fervor.

Fight or Flight

Now, the plot thickens. A large, healthy buck feeling the power of his scraping efforts on the woodland floor, smelling where a doe actually visited *his* scrape — and, then another buck shows up.

At this point each buck faces the basic situation of nature's "fight or flight" plan. Wildlife researchers note that weight and age are highly correlated, and the oldest and heaviest buck typically wins the battle and breeds the doe. An old buck, say ten or twelve years old and past his prime, usually would not have the stamina to win, however. Such aged bucks may have to "stand in line," relenting to their younger offspring.

This fighting ritual is critical to herd survival because it involves genetics, genetics in terms of strength, adaptation to the environ-

During an actual fight between two bucks vying for dominance, there is much clacking, grinding, and grating of antler tines as they engage their headgear. The hunter who can imitate this sound may well cause other large bucks to come in to investigate. Rattling is best done with another hunting partner who watches for the buck's approach as well as for other hunters who may hear the sound (Drawing by Dixie Holcomb)

ment, and internal physiology. So, it is biologically important that the winner breeds the doe.

During an actual battle, there is much clashing, crunching, and grinding of calcified antlers. The grating sound often carries to the ears of another interested buck. Other bucks are attracted to the fight, knowing that a prize is up for grabs and that they might get in on the act. Or, perhaps, they just want to see a good show.

At any rate, they will likely come running to investigate, making the rattling of antlers a worthwhile technique for the deer hunter in attracting bucks toward his stand.

The animal kingdom is "red in tooth and claw" and fraught with conflict. For the fighting bucks during the rut, such is both the pleasure and plight of their being.

Structured within the sperm and egg of each individual buck and doe are those characteristics that determine deer survival through time, as predators, hunters, and starvation prey upon the herd.

Thus, as far as the perpetuation of white-tailed deer, their survival depends upon the best genetic stock doing the breeding. "Best" in this case means the production of that theoretical deer that can evade all predators, survive winters and droughts on minimum and varied food sources, ward off diseases and parasites, live to a ripe old age, and annually enter the breeding cycle.

Consequently, the internal hormonal activity, the attacking of shrubs, the digging of scrapes in the earth, and the clash of racks between fighting bucks, all help assure that the white-tailed deer keep populating its niche.

Like other sensationalized heroes in our society, the buck with a big rack has become romanticized by the hunter. Like the medieval knight and the American cowboy, our image of the hero often becomes greater than it is in real life.

Enter, then, the hunter who rolls out of the bed at three o'clock in the morning, dresses in camouflage to look like a tree, grabs his compound bow, scratches the frost from the windshield of his battered pickup truck, drives forty miles through the predawn cold, and climbs a tree with much grunting and wormlike movements, obsessed, but happily so, with this romanticized mystique of a trophy buck.

So, luckily for the deer hunter, bucks have made their masculine challenges within the social hierarchy of the herd. Arrogantly through their domain, attempting to take on all others, they go, relenting only to a more dominant buck. This is nature's method for survival.

Chapter 8

Deer Communication

The Alert Whitetail

The white-tailed deer receives messages through his nervous system from the environment. Deer, like man, have five senses: the ability to hear, see, taste, feel, and smell. Moreover, these messages are interpreted by the deer's brain, and decisions are made based upon what it smelled, saw, or heard.

Deer do learn from their life experiences. Even though the cerebrum (top, front) portion of the deer's brain is not as well developed as man's, deer do have the ability to remember. A deer does remember where along their trail it saw a hunter who made a slight metallic sound with his bow or gun. Because of that experience, the deer may change his trail pattern.

Sometimes a hunter may be lucky enough to locate an extremely active deer trail. From a position high up in a tree stand, he may observe several deer moving over this trail. During the late summer and early fall, droughts are common over parts of the United States. Often, then, the bow hunter during early season hunts may locate his tree-stand close to the deer's watering hole.

The white-tailed deer has highly developed senses. A keen ability to smell is the deer's main line of defense. Deer also have good seeing and hearing ability, as demonstrated by this young doe in a winterland environment.

Under such conditions the bow hunter has a good chance to harvest deer. However, in the process, several deer will soon learn the hunter's location. For instance, three or four deer may be walking in single file along the trail leading to the water hole. The hunter, in order to take his deer, must make the critical decision of when to release his arrow and send it on its flight. In doing so, the hunter is naturally going to startle some of the deer. And, the deer that escaped remembers that event and where it occurred.

When undisturbed, deer walk their trails, perhaps a mile or so in warm weather, as a daily routine. Further, the deer often pass certain points along their trail near the same time each day. The hunter who can figure out these daily trail habits greatly enhances his chances of success.

Scents and Vocalizations

When startled, deer evidently do emit scents from the glands between their toes. Thus, when other deer walk the same trail and smell these fear-induced scents, they become more wary. The whitetail leaves both visual and scent markings that act as signposts to other deer in the area. Fecal droppings, pheromonal deposits, urinary deposits, and other scent marks are common over the whitetail's trails. And, as cattle do, the whitetail has the habit of trail following. By doing so, deer burn less energy than when constantly breaking new trails. Also, it is simply a mental habit for animals to follow trails, man included.

Often the hunter may find active deer trails a foot wide where several deer have walked, usually in single file. In walking single file over their trails, deer communicate several messages to the deer with them. By casual tail-flicking, a deer lets the others behind know that all is well and no predators have been spotted.

In this fashion the whitetail moves cautiously over his trails. Stopping and going, looking for predators and signaling is the whitetail's workaday world. This habit serves both to conserve their energy and to spot any possible danger. When approaching suspected danger or new objects, the whitetail's demeanor changes drastically. Now, with head, ears, and tail erect, he is a bundle of potential energy, communicating to other deer all around that something is wrong. Even deer in front may see the alerted deer's

Deer have scent glands between their toes and upon their legs. The glands are accentuated externally by tufts of hair as shown on this young deer's back legs. When startled, deer emit a scent from these glands that serves to warn other deer.

white throat patch and know that they, too, should look for possible danger.

A deer's general demeanor, then, is an effective communicator to other deer. It is for this reason that deer traveling in single file over trails are so hard to fool by hunters. To the hunter it seems that at least one deer is looking around all the time in order to communicate a startle-response to other members of the group.

Although deer cannot vocalize in the sense that man can, deer do send vocal communications. It is now known that the whitetail can make about twelve meaningful vocal sounds.

The most prevalent sound encountered by the hunter is a deer's alerting snort. Both bucks and does may snort and alert other deer when scenting a predator. But, when snorting, the deer may not necessarily know the hunter's exact location. Thus, immobility by the hunter is important upon hearing the deer's snort. Just possibly the deer may still pass within range.

When caught, sometimes when wounded, deer make a distress call. This high-pitched sound communicated to other deer makes them highly alerted. A fawn distress call will sometimes bring deer into an area, especially does. Deer calls that simulate the fawn's high-pitched bleating are used by hunters to attract deer. These calls are sold commercially and resemble a duck call in appearance.

Deer communicate to other deer where food, salt, and water are located. Paw marks and nibbled-on vegetative shoots communicate to any deer what other herd members are eating. Thus, salt licks, acorns, mushrooms, and other edibles are visual signs of deer usage. The same visual signs, of course, are valuable to the hunter.

Whitetails often walk in single file while ambling over their trails. By casual side-to-side tail-flicking movements, they communicate that no danger is present. The hunter, then, should be aware of a whitetail's general demeanor before making his shot, especially an arrow release.

During the peak of the rut, bucks make a vocalized grunt while looking for does. This vocal message to does in the area lets them know of the buck's sexual intentions. During the buck's rut, the hunter should listen for this piglike sound. Upon hearing it, the hunter's slow, deliberate movement with his firearm toward a shooting lane may mean zeroing-in on a trophy buck.

Deer in the wild have several reasons to communicate their intentions. Their communicative signals usually revolve around the search for food, signaling danger, doe-fawn affection, peer group play, dominance display, and the sexual drive between rutting bucks and estrous does in heat.

Although visual and vocal signals are used by deer in the wild to a great extent, scent making is one of their most effective means of communication. During the rut, a buck's hormonal and sexual systems are running at their peak. Sexual pheromones then from the estrous doe's urinary tract stimulates the limbic, pleasure-evoking part of the buck's brain. This part of an animal's brain is responsible for stimulating his active sexual drives and expressions. The doe's sexual pheromones carried on the air currents communicate her drives and intentions to the buck.

Sexual Communication

To further inundate the moist sensitive tissues within his nostrils with the pheromones, the buck curls back his upper lip and pulls the air currents over it. This sexual activity is called Flehmen, or lip-curl. While following or actually in close contact with does, the buck may be seen performing Flehmen, which intensifies his sexual arousal. Pheromone-based lures bought commercially by the hunter and applied near his hunting stand are effective. The buck, if he doesn't sense the hunter, may well think that he is on the trail of an estrous doe in heat.

Furthermore, at the buck's scrapes, the doe deposits pheromones in her urine, the buck performs Flehmen there, too. The scrape is an active point of communication to other deer in the area, also. Other bucks may smell the scrape and try to take it over and become the dominant buck. Thus, the buck's competitive messages are communicated by the scrape, as more that one buck may try to use it in looking for does that are attracted.

During the rut bucks spend a lot of time aggressively seeking out sexual pheromone deposits made by does. Then false scrapes and pheromone canisters may be used to lure bucks near a hunter's stand. These are effective luring techniques, and many hunters now use them.

Does locate not only bucks but also their fawns by both olfactory and visual efforts. Fawns travel very little for a month or so immediately following their birth. The doe leaves her fawns well camouflaged in the forest as safe as possible from predators. The doe's time is then spent browsing and bedding before returning to the fawns for suckling.

Under ideal browsing conditions, the doe will typically bear two fawns and place them about a hundred yards apart. Separated, the fawns are not tempted to play at their early age and attract predators. Thus, upon the doe's return, she remembers the scent of her separate fawns and locates them. However, it is known that for the first three weeks of its life, the fawn gives off little detectable scent to other animals. This little trick of nature's enables the fawn to avoid predators during its most vulnerable time.

It is understood, then, that visual, auditory, and olfactory communications is just as important to the deer as to the hunter. Consequently, while deer hunting you have to pay constant attention to these acute abilities.

Browsing, sexual reproduction by the buck and doe, care of fawns by the doe, and establishment of dominance by both bucks and does constitutes much of the life-supporting activities of the whitetailed deer. All of these necessary survival functions depend upon effective communication. In certain of these efforts, the whitetail is far superior to man.

Man, of course, depends upon his technological advances to outwit the deer. Further, man understands his technology and deer do not. It is for this reason then that deer have trouble in object interpretation. The hunter understands the different sounds associated with moving machinery, motors, and other technological devices.

The whitetail, however, has evolved in evading predators. Admittedly, deer sometimes seem to do unexpected things. But a fawn, after living only a few days in the wild with its mother, has devel-

Stands or any other objects that the hunter intends to use during the hunting season should be built before opening day so deer can become accustomed to them.

oped the evasive instinct that is so necessary for its survival. The doe communicates to the fawn that new objects over their trails are to be treated with suspect.

Any permanent stand that the hunter intends to use during the hunting season, therefore, should be constructed well in advance of its intended use. The hunter then gives the deer time to get used to it. Otherwise, the deer will be wary of the stand and communicate their fear and demeanor to other deer in the hunting area.

Chapter 9

The Rutting Season

Cold Weather Breeding Responses

The white-tailed buck is a seasonally cyclic animal in his sexual activities. Consequently, each winter the buck experiences the sexual impulse to breed. This is called the rut.

Prior to the actual rut, the buck goes through a series of physiological events that prepare him for this important time.

During spring and summer the buck has likely been running with another buck or two or in small bachelor groups. In doing so, they have browsed and grown fat on green plants. In July the bucks' antlers grow fast, almost half an inch on some days. In the summer, the bucks live together peacefully and store up energy in the form of body fat that is deposited in areas other than the muscles, which are practically fat-free.

During this summer-browsing, fattening, and antler-growing phase, the bucks run a daily pattern in browsing, bedding, visiting a watering hole, and resting together just off their browsing sites.

Over the midwestern woodlot section of the United States, bucks bed down adjacent to where beef cattle graze or farmers grow their crops. In summer, one may roust up small groups of bucks which are only a few yards deep in a woodland that is adjacent to farmland. White-tailed deer, both bucks and does, are creatures of the break areas. Both sexes spend a lot of time browsing or standing in open spaces adjacent to cover. Here, within three or four seconds, the deer can run into thick cover that protects them from view.

As fall approaches, however, the buck's racks finish growing, and the velvet starts to shed. Further, bucks that travel in groups notice their neighbors' racks. Intuitively, then the bucks place themselves in an order of dominance based upon their body and rack sizes. No fighting with racks occurs during the summer, however, because the developing antlers are tender and sensitive to the touch. Nerves that carry touch sensations and blood vessels that carry carbohydrates, proteins, and dissolved minerals constitute part of the antlers before final growth and hardening occur.

All of this physiological preparation is necessary before the rut takes place. Bucks are in a different physiological state in summer as opposed to their condition in winter during the rut. Specifically, in spring and summer, the buck's sperm count is at its lowest. During early summer a buck generally could not breed a doe even if the impulse occurred to him. Thus, the hormonal production within the buck's body keeps him on nature's course, to do his breeding during the late fall and early winter.

As fall approaches, the buck's antlers, covered with velvet, reach their full growth and spread dimensions. Late-summer scouting is important to the hunter. For after once locating a trophy-racked buck, a hunter will at least know a portion of the buck's home range. It is necessary, however, for a hunter to figure out the buck's pattern later during the winter hunting season, when food sources, hunting pressure, and natural factors such as temperatures and snowfall affect the deer's daily routine.

Full hardening of a buck's antlers is followed by shedding of the velvet covering. Nerve impulses and blood supplies to the velvet gradually cease. The antlers then consist of dead, solidified minerals and are as strong and heavy as so much concrete. The antlers at this point, even though matured and solidified, are still biologically active where they attach to the buck's skull. In late winter or in early spring, the pedicel area of attachment, however, will weaken, and the buck will lose his annual rack.

When antler growth ceases prior to the rut, the buck will strip the velvet covering from his rack by rubbing it against saplings and small trees. At first the velvet still contains remnants of blood vessels that once actively fed the live antlers. The first rub attempts break these vessels and cause an initial, red coloring of coagulated blood over the buck's antlers.

Still prior to the rut, say in mid to late fall, the buck with his new headgear battles many bushes over his home range. Scouting then and finding rub marks on these saplings signal that bucks are definitely in the area, for no other creature is likely to make such an emblazoned mark two feet high or so on several saplings.

By rubbing prior to the rut, the buck not only tears the velvet from his antlers but also strengthens his neck muscles. The buck now carries around his strong, insensitive rack. Now quite heavy, the rack requires strength to bear. Thus, the sapling-whipping routine is quite important in preparing the buck's neck muscles for future battles with other bucks. For then both strength and stamina are called upon in head-to-head combat with other strong competitors.

The buck is fattened on summer browse and has reserve fat stored beneath his backbone. His neck muscles bulge, and a sleek coat of heavy winter hair covers his body. The new polished rack adorning his head make him a formidable warrior indeed. Nature has prepared and honed the buck to breed and reproduce his kind.

The buck in rut is strong and lustful and roams his home range in search of does in heat. The buck in rut, should he be large and well-racked, trades saplings for larger timber. The scouting hunter then, to his own satisfaction, may find trees up to a foot or so in diameter with shredded bark three feet above the ground.

Depending upon latitude over the United States, the bucks go into rut during late fall or early winter. Demeanor, agility, age, and overall stamina are important factors as the bucks establish their order of dominance prior to and during the rut. In other words, the oldest and largest buck is not *always* the dominant one. Willpower and determination also become critical factors in fighting and subsequent breeding of the does.

Solitary bucks form scrapes about two to three feet in diameter during the peak of the rut. On the forest floor they paw into the dirt with their front hooves. This scrape is usually made quite close to a

During the rutting season, dominant bucks break from their bachelor groups and become more solitary in nature. These bucks then search for does to breed, making woodland scrapes to attract does. Trophy hunting is better during the rut because the larger bucks do more rambling, are more obvious around scrapes, and are less cautious then.

small sapling with an overhanging branch three or four feet above the ground. Near the base of this sapling, the rutting buck makes his scrape, urinates upon his tarsal glands on his legs to increase the scent within the scrape, and rubs more glandular scent upon the branches immediately above the scrape. Upon these twigs, the buck uses glandular scent from his preorbital eye glands and the glands at the base of his antlers. Then he may spread the secretions with his tongue.

The purpose of these glandular deposits made by the buck, of course, is to attract a doe in heat. During the rut, the buck makes several such scrapes over his home range. Sometimes along break areas such as trails where bulldozers have engaged in previous logging operations, a rutting buck makes several scrapes in a line. Often at intermittent distances of thirty to forty yards or so, scrapes extend for 150 yards or more.

Hunter Application

In a tree stand, then, the hunter can climb about mid-distance along this scrape line and watch the entire area for the buck as he freshens his scrapes and looks for does. Does, while in sexual heat, are just as interested in finding the bucks as the bucks are in locating them. Thus, a buck's primary scrape does increase deer traffic in an area.

Rain, snow, and falling leaves disperse and degrade the glandular scents left by the buck at his scrape. Thus, following a rain or snow the buck will often freshen his primary scrapes and paw, once again, his urinary deposits into the moistened earth. After pawing around in these deposits, the buck will purposefully track the contents along his trail. This deliberate action by the buck further increases the doe's possibility of contacting him.

Upon locating the buck's scrape, should the buck not be present, the doe urinates within the scrape and deposits her pheromones. Further, the doe trails these pheromones into the woods a short distance as she leaves the scrape. The pheromones from her urinary tract are powerful sexual stimulants. They are carried by the wind and disperse. The buck, by sniffing the wind currents with his sensitive nostrils, is able to locate the doe in heat.

When the buck returns to his scrape, the doe, still lingering, will sometimes dash off into the woods. Typically, however, her actions are circular and really go nowhere, in a sense, except to further entice the buck. Once again an old adage is true: "The boy chases the girl until she catches him." The doe, if in heat, only runs in circles until the buck breeds her.

But should the doe not be in heat, but her monthly estrous cycle is fast approaching, she may run quite a long distance with the buck in pursuit. When this happens, the buck sometimes pursues her for miles and actually leaves his normal home range. The doe, in effect, sets the territorial boundary for the buck during the rut. The rut is one of the few times that a buck is known to leave his home range.

Moreover, when rutting, the buck does not follow his normal reclusive routines as closely. Instead of bedding up during the day and staying hidden, the buck becomes much more conspicious over the forest. With stored fat from summer browse, his hormonal activity at a peak, and his breeding impulse at an annual high, the buck becomes much more aggressive. So while in rut, the buck eats less, sleeps less, and rambles more. The hunter who then does the same may just cross the buck's path and collect a trophy.

The hunter can buy doe-in-heat lure containing pheromonal extracts, place it in empty thirty-five millimeter film canisters filled with cotton, and set the containers, about a foot above the ground, at choice spots in his hunting area near his tree stand.

Ideally, the hunter should find a well-used deer trail during his scouting and climb in his tree stand over this trail. Just before climbing, the hunter then opens a film canister filled with the doe-in-rut extract on cotton. The sexual pheromones, thus exposed to the air, do draw deer to the area and hold them for a while. A buck thinks that, once again, he has found a doe in heat when he smells the commercial pheromones.

Does also notice these pheromone lures and react to them. Some hunters, however, report that small, young does appear nervous around these pheromone deposits. This point still needs researching. Possibly, young and less dominant does are repulsed or intimidated by larger ones.

Many hunters apply the doe-in-rut contents to a rag and drag it the last 100 yards or so before climbing into their stand. Also, the opened doe-in-rut contents are set about ten yards away in a shooting lane that a buck will hopefully use. Other hunters also walk

Does are in sexual heat during the late fall and winter. Bucks may extend their home range during the rut in pursuing does. Does that are not bred during one estrous cycle may breed about 28 days later during their next cycle. Wintertime sexual activities of the whitetail increases the hunter's chances of bagging a deer. (Drawing by Dixie Holcomb)

around their stand and drag the doe-in-rut contents on a rag. This pools the sexual pheromones within the hunter's immediate area. Even though the doe's sexual pheromones are chemically light enough to disperse on wind currents, they are molecularly heavy enough to linger for a few hours.

On primitive weapons hunts, in which the deer hunter may harvest either bucks or does, this method may be used successfully, since the larger does, at least, are attracted to these sexual deposits.

Another hunter technique used to attract a rutting buck is the making of an artificial scrape. In such practice, the hunter marks up the forest floor with a stick or some tool. After making these marks, the hunter places a drip bottle of doe-in-rut lure several feet above the artificial scrape. Here, from a shrub limb, the bottle drips slowly into the marked area. The slowly dripping bottle of doe-in-rut solution keeps the artificial scrape continually fresh in sexual pheromones that may carry to the sensitive nose of a buck.

The theory behind the hunter making an artificial scrape is that the dominant buck in the area will take it over, even though he may not have been the first buck to find it. Some hunters swear by this method as a good trophy hunting technique.

When the hunter makes the artificial scrape, he must be careful not to contaminate the scrape area with his human scent. It is advisable for the hunter to wear rubber gloves while working around the scrape. Further, as in all deer hunting, rubber-soled boots are best to wear when marking up the forest floor and simulating the paw marks that a buck would normally make. Some hunters also carry plastic sheets to stand and walk upon around the artificial scrape area.

After setting up the artificial scrape, the hunter then later climbs into his tree stand near the scrape. Then, according to the theory, the dominant buck will eventually use the scrape as his own while running off lesser competitor bucks. By this practice, a hunter hopes to harvest the dominant buck in the area. Bucks do recognize the scent of other bucks and know where they stand in the pecking order. Thus, a buck that appears nervous or is reluctant to approach the artificial scrape or to paw and urinate in it is probably not the dominant buck in the immediate area.

As the rutting period progresses through the winter, most of the does are bred. Wildlife biologists have found that near ninety-five percent of all does within an area will be bred before the rut ends. Does generally can be bred during a five-month period over the fall and winter. The does come into sexual heat on a 28-day cycle. Thus a doe that is not bred in any particular cycle may be bred during her next heat cycle.

The dominant rutting bucks are run ragged by the end of their rut period. Many lose fifteen to twenty percent of their body weight, as they eat less and spend much time in giving attention to the does coming into estrus. Also, time and effort is spent in maintaining

The hunter may harvest bigger bucks during the rut. Rutting bucks often form their scrape lines along woodland trails and break areas that loggers have used.

their scrape lines and reinforcing their dominant status with subordinate bucks that may, however, challenge with their own headgear.

It is common during the rutting period for a hunter to harvest bucks that have obviously been in several battles. Upon the buck's shoulder and neck the hunter finds gouge marks where another buck has cut the first with his antler tines.

At the end of the rut — about January or February at the latest for most latitudes — the antler base at the buck's skull becomes weak. The hardened antlers then fall upon the forest floor and are soon eaten by rodents that feed upon the mineral content.

The buck's role in the reproductive process has then been completed. His whole demeanor changes as he is now without headgear that may be used in pushing contests with other bucks. The buck is also different internally. His sperm production drops back to a nonbreeding level, and his hormonal system now starts to gear up for new antler growth.

Moreover, when the new vegetative growth of spring arrives, the buck starts packing on some more weight. He soon gains back the weight loss that occurred during the last rut. Plus, the buck adds a few more pounds to his weight of the preceding year until he is about seven and a half years old, if nutrition is adequate. So, as the years go by, the buck will maintain his dominant status for a few years, perhaps. But, if not harvested by the hunter, the buck will decline near his ninth year as his teeth wear out and he can no longer maintain the energy, poundage, agility, and stamina to run his scrape lines and fight off other aspiring young bucks that are eager to breed the does. In the end, then, nature sees to it that the best-fit bucks breed the does.

Chapter 10

The Role of the Doe

Does in the Whitetail Social Order

Much time is spent by deer hunters in discussions about bucks. But in perpetuating the species, of course, the doe is just as important as the buck.

Since the early beginnings of our country, many hunters have been reluctant to harvest does. In James Fenimore Cooper's classic novel, *The Deerslayer*, published in 1841, the frontiersman, Deerslayer, asked Chingachgook, his Indian friend, if he had ever killed a doe, implying, of course, that he shouldn't have.

Under present-day game management policies, the deer herd population must be regulated to the carrying capacity of the land. Otherwise, starvation and disease will strike the herd. Further, when an area becomes greatly overbrowsed, winter die-offs often cut the herd drastically. Once they occur, these die-offs cut the herd back well below the carrying capacity. Thus, these life-death cycles control the whitetail populations.

Under correct game management policies, though, the hunter is permitted to help regulate the deer herd population. Consequently,

Alert does are the teachers of young deer. They teach their fawns to evade predators, to search for seasonal foods, and to be wary of new objects within their home range. The doe's alert manner and raised white flag are messages to her fawns.

it becomes necessary to harvest does in order to permit more deer to live over the game management acreage in the long-run.

In the social order of the deer family, the doe both nourishes and teaches the young fawns. Fawns that are taken from the doe only a day or two after birth and raised by man become tame and fail to exhibit their wild behavior to the fullest extent. Such a deer becomes modified in his behavior pattern. Furthermore, were such a tame deer suddenly released into the wild, he would soon run into trouble from predators and probably be killed.

For natural survival of deer over time, it is necessary for the doe to render her important training to the fawns. Moreover, immediately following birth it is important that the fawn suckle the doe and receive disease immunities from her milk. This should be accomplished even if the fawn is removed for taming. Thus, by suckling, nuzzling, and licking the fawn, the doe causes the fawns intestinal tract and system to receive the necessary bacteria needed for its digestive and immunity functions.

For a month or so following birth, the camouflaged fawn lies more or less immobile within the woodland. Then after gaining a few pounds, along with consequent speed and agility, the fawn follows the doe over trails. Here the fawn learns the wild nature that is so necessary for its survival. The fawn soon learns the stop-and-go trail-walking technique coupled with much standing and looking that is important in detecting danger. With its keen nose the fawn soon learns the smell of predators. Then, when the fawn sees the doe go into a tail-flaring run, it learns to do the same.

The Doe Teaches the Fawn

This teaching phase, of course, occurs from about June through September each year. At this time the doe is dominant within the social group, because the buck has new, tender antlers and cannot fight with other deer. So, the doe literally kicks the buck around and maintains family dominance.

Large does within the group are the dominant ones, too. The various, small deer groups have a dominant doe that leads the group through the woods and over the trails. The hunter, then, from his tree stand usually sees the dominant doe first. From a tree stand, the hunter's first indication of deer traffic, moving over dried leaves and twigs, is often the crunch-crunch sound made by the lead doe. This crunching sound is often rhythmic and denotes that a large animal is moving through the forest. This may be the bow hunter's initial signal to nock his arrow, shift his body deliberately and noiselessly toward the designated shooting lane, and get ready to draw his bow.

This one important sequence is the most critical in hunting. Any ill-fated mistake by the hunter cannot be corrected should he startle the deer. Also, deer will likely remember where the hunter startled them, and the lead doe will choose a different trail pattern. The fawns learn from these early close encounters, and the wild state of alertness is perpetuated.

Fawns are born about seven months after the breeding of the doe during the rutting season in cold weather. Deer protoplasm, the developing material for future deer generations, is carried through the harsh winters within the body of the doe. Even though the cold weather along with high winds may drive the chill factor to nearly 100° below zero, the developing fetus is maintained at a constantly warm and comfortable body temperature within the womb of the doe.

Timely Breeding of the Doe

Conception of the does on a timely basis, then, is of ultimate importance for survival of fawns. Generally does can breed from October through February; however, most breeding occurs during November, December, or January, depending on the latitude from north to south. Over the states near the Canadian border, the rut with subsequent breeding of the doe occurs in November. At the latitude of Atlanta, Georgia, the rut is usually in late December. A doe that is bred in November will drop her fawn in June amid the lush green vegetation of the beginning summer growth.

Since the dominant doe is the trail boss, much well-being of the deer family depends upon her efforts. Location of seasonal food sources, knowing escape routes from predators, and sexually attracting the buck during the rut are all life-supporting functions performed by the doe.

Fertile does lactate and give milk during the summer while the fawns suckle. As winter approaches, though, milk production by the doe drops to zero. Bow hunters in the fall often find lactating does while field-dressing harvested deer. The gun hunter in winter, however, is not likely to do so, because by December and January the doe has stopped milk production entirely.

This stoppage of milk production serves two purposes, both necessary for long-range whitetail survival. First, by wintertime the fawn must be taught to be food-independent of the doe. Sub-zero temperatures are not conducive to either the fawn's wet muzzle or the doe's wet udder. Suckling also takes away attention that could better be devoted to looking for predators. Further, it slows escape attempts by the doe and fawn.

Second, the doe must conserve her own energy resources during winter. Physiologically, in the wintertime, whitetail deer go into a

Fawns are weaned before wintertime and taught to be doe-independent. Yet, young fawns in the wild follow the doe and learn to react to her evasive nature. Fawns raised by man from birth fail to fully exhibit their wild nature.

much reduced energy state. They do not hibernate, but they do cut food consumption, reduce their home range rambling to about one-tenth of the summer distance, bed, and move much less over their home range. Thus, in this reduced energy state, the doe does not produce milk and makes every attempt to conserve her energy as a protection against cold weather. In short, the calories that the doe burns go toward maintaining her own body temperature in winter-time survival.

Early Summer Fawning Promotes Survival

Here we can see the importance of well-timed fawning dates in relation to herd survival. In the long run in cold climates, it is

The development of trophy racks is affected by herd genetics. Smaller does and spike bucks are best harvested in game management practices. Here, Paul McBride is shown with a spike buck that he took while bow hunting in Alabama. Alabama and Mississippi now have more than a million whitetails. Game management policies permit the harvesting of one buck per day for any hunter who is so lucky.

mandatory that fawns be born in early summer so that they can suckle, grow, and wean from the doe's milk before the harshness of winter strikes. In short, any spotted fawns going into the grip of winter are automatically pressed for survival. His food sources are restricted, predators have the advantage in any deep snow, and the fawn's body mass is not great enough to sustain energy production against lowered, wintertime temperatures and winds.

Summer fawning dates are ultimately governed by the winter rut and breeding, since about 210 days separate the two natural events. Sexual activity by the doe in heat is important during the cold-season rut. Much deer activity and attention then is centered around the buck's scrapes. This important signal by the buck for the doe is also important for the deer hunter. Scrape hunting, the placing of one's stand near this increased deer activity pattern, does increase the hunter's chances of harvesting a dominant buck — which, by the very process, selects out the healthier, larger bucks with the bigger racks.

Wintertime sexual pheromone secretion by the doe in heat then becomes an important and critical phenomenon for whitetail survival. The reason is, of course, that breeding must be well-timed so that fawning will occur within the typical 189- to 222-day range.

Further, the natural urge for power and dominance causes the bucks to fight and vie for the doe's sexual favors. The whole process is nature's way of promoting a healthy fawn at the right time of the year when ample food is available for the doe and her fawn.

Any ill-timed breeding then foils this well-designed natural plan. Thus, does go out of estrus in February if not bred, and the buck's racks are cast about the same time. Also, the buck's sperm count decreases to below breeding capacity. These coordinated processes greatly reduce the chances of poorly timed breeding and subsequent fawning.

Good herd genetics that are responsible for producing trophy bucks come from the does as well as from the bucks. Even though does generally do not grow antlers — only rarely through hormonal imbalances — they do bear genetic traits that affect rack size of their male offspring.

In good game management policies, older spike bucks as well as smaller adult does are best removed to promote the future chances for larger bucks with trophy racks.

Chapter 11

The Fawn

Gestation Period

The rut, centering near the buck's scrapes and hotly pursued by the deer hunters around December, culminates in one or more fawns in summer. The deer hunter, through all of his trial and error in trying to fool a whitetail deer, learns that timing is important. Effective use of firearms and equipment, while remaining as quiet as possible, is mandatory in becoming a successful hunter. Ultimately, then, fractions of seconds and inches determine whether one's arrow or bullet was well placed in bringing down a deer.

Similarly, the whitetail's life habits are timed precisely as a result of evolutionary development in harsh environments. In the cold reaches of his range, the whitetail pulls through showing his best characteristics in larger racks, greater body weights, and precision in rutting and subsequent fawning.

Following the breeding of the doe, the length of time that the developing fetus spends within the uterus is called the gestation period. A correctly timed gestation period that nourishes the fetus through cold, inclement weather greatly enhances survival of whitetailed deer in northern latitudes.

Fawns are hard-pressed for survival their first winter, as they struggle to survive the ravaging cold, wind, and snow. Greater body mass of fawns born early in the summer gives them a survival advantage.

The comfort range for whitetails ranges from 41°F to 68°F. Fawns, however, on a starvation diet show severe stress at air temperatures near 32°F and a wind velocity of one mile per hour and less. But a fawn on a nutritious diet can withstand winter exposure to 40°F below zero, with a wind velocity of eight miles per hour. The fawn's first winter, then, is a critical point in its life. Until the ravages of old age set in, a deer's first winter is its most severe test.

Thus, fawns which are underdeveloped or dropped too close to winter usually have a hard go of it. During the rut, most of the does become pregnant, but when hard-pressed by lack of food, the mortality rate of their fawns is often quite high. Most fawn deaths happen shortly after birth, during the first two or three weeks, because the young deer was poorly developed within its mother's womb. Also, it has been shown that even healthy fawns gain very little weight from December through April. As a yearling the following summer, though, young deer grow rapidly when browse is plentiful.

Late-season spotted fawns may be a signal that the herd is hard-pressed for food and that proper herd reduction through increased hunter harvest should be made. Healthy does fawn earlier, on the average, than do does on poor browse. If the doe is in prime health, living in an area with abundant and nutritious browse, fawn birth dates are usually ten to twelve days earlier than for those born to less robust does. Other natural variables, such as the amount of spring rainfall, also contribute to early fawning. But, directly, the good health of the doe is primarily responsible for most early fawning.

The long-range result of a doe in heat during the period of the rut, found and bred by a buck, is a seven-pound fawn. This timely breeding enables the doe to provide the suckling fawn with ample, energy-rich milk, and within six weeks the youngster is in good condition and looking for green vegetation on his own.

Does remain in sexual heat for approximately twenty-four hours during their monthly estrous cycles. Thus, sexual pheromone attraction by bucks becomes critically important for the does. It is necessary that the doe in heat be quickly found by the rutting buck. Doe-in-rut sexual lures have a sound scientific basis and have proven more effective than food-scented lures. The rutting buck is much more interested in breeding the does than in looking for acorns, for example.

Dominant bucks going into the rut with fat packed along their spines from abundant fall vegetative browse do not spend much time eating. For about two months or so during the rut, the bucks eat very little while reacting greatly to any pheromonal sexual dispersal by the does.

Does which are not bred repeat their short heat cycles on a lunar cycle, the name so derived from the moon, which repeats its different phases every twenty-eight days. Here, it may be noticed how animals on earth, in this case the whitetailed deer, have been influenced over the course of their own evolution by natural forces acting upon them and their environment.

In February pregnant does sometimes have difficulty in finding adequate food to support the developing fawn within them. The final three months of the gestation period are the most critical for the unborn fawn. Failure of the doe to receive adequate food then usually results in a small fawn that does not survive.

Body Mass for Cold Weather

Formed during the gestation period, body weight, shape, and body proportions are important to a fawn's survival. For example, long, spindly legs are soon called upon to evade predators, but not to escape the winter cold. A relatively small body-surface area relative to body mass is important in protecting the fawn's vitals zone from the winter chill. Older, heavier fawns born in early summer have a greater body-mass to body-surface ratio during their first winter than newborn fawns before growth and weight gains.

The doe-fawn relationship is important to the hunter because it relates directly to future trail patterns for the young deer. The bow hunter, say on a late-September hunt, is well accustomed to observing older fawns following the doe over their trails. The fawns learn these home-range trail patterns early in life, of course, and retain them later without the presence of the doe, perhaps. Thus, the hunter can be reasonably assured that once he finds major whitetail trails, crossings, and runways that these same patterns will be followed again.

Sure, the whitetails alter some of their trail patterns according to

Biological timing is critical in a whitetail's life. For long-range herd survival it is important that the does are bred quickly during the rut. Then fawns are born early and have enough body mass to survive their first winter. (Drawing by Dixie Holcomb)

the seasons, food supplies, water, herd density, social dominance, air temperatures, weather, terrain alterations, and hunting pressure. However, deer seldom leave their home range for any extended length of time. Consequently, after the fawns once learn their home range trail patterns from the doe, they tend to continue using at least a major portion of the main runways and escape routes.

For the hunter, then, seasonal scouting is time well spent. The hunter's observation and mental notes of water holes, oak flats, honeysuckle patches, cedar thickets, canebrakes, terrain features, ravines, draws, ridges, creeks, bulldozer trails, breakpoints, meadows, and adjacent farm crops all figure into the whitetail's movement patterns.

Within the whitetail's general home range radius of one and a half miles, the deer may toss the hunter many change-up pitches in trail alterations. However, that home range radius is still a relatively small living area for a big-game animal, and the trail patterns are taught to each succeeding fawn by the doe.

The gestation period for deer is about one-fourth less than the gestation time for people — near seven months in deer. Man evolved and adapted to care for and house his offspring through the winter. The deer's best option, however, is for the doe to carry the youngster within her body during the winter.

In summary, nature, through the ages of animal evolution, pressured and selected the white-tailed deer to breed in late fall or early winter and fawn in the summer in the temperate regions on earth. These precise natural events in the deer's life are hormonally regulated and triggered over the northern latitudes mainly by daylength, the photoperiod. As a final result the whitetail's breeding and fawning dates are very close to the winter and summer solstices: the shortest and the longest days in the year.

Wildlife scientists have demonstrated in laboratory experiments that the fawn's genetic material, the chromosomes, half of which are received from the buck in his sperm and half from the doe in her egg, are subject to more variable change than the sperm and egg material from other warm-blooded animals. This potential for change provides the whitetail with his great adaptability for survival when stalked by his predators, including the hunter. These internally adaptable traits passed on from generation to generation enables whitetail to live in a small home-range area undetected by many would-be predators.

Chapter 12

Home Range
for Whitetails

Small Home Range

The white-tailed deer is a homebody. He does not free-roam. Instead, the whitetail chooses an area of land about one and a half miles in radius and lives there. For the hunter, then, this knowledge is important. After once locating a big buck, a hunter can be quite assured that his prize trophy will at least be close by.

The whitetail's home range is not necessarily circular in shape, however. Since deer characteristically follow both new and well-worn trails, the whitetail's home range is often elliptical. This oblong configuration stems from the whitetail running a generalized trail pattern over the length of his home range. Spur side trips to watering holes, bedding areas, and seasonally changing food sources form the geometric borders to the whitetail's elliptical-shaped home-range quarters.

Generally, the white-tailed deer has adapted more to the eastern two-thirds of the United States. Here, among the Appalachian Mountains, the southern highlands and swamps, the eastern woodlots, the midwestern farm lands, the Canadian border states, and along the length of the Mississippi River Delta, the whitetail has evolved to seek protective cover over a relatively small home range. In scientific description, *Odocoileus virginianus*, the eastern white-tailed deer, is an evolutionary first cousin to *Odocoileus hemionus*, the western mule deer.

The mule deer, even as a fawn, is more migratory in nature than a newborn whitetail. Research studies show that a mule deer fawn buck moves around in his daily activities more than does a white-tailed fawn buck. These data, of course, indicate that, genetically, the two species have evolved characteristic differences in enhancing survival in each of their respective habitats.

These basic genetic differences relate directly to deer hunting techniques and equipment usage. Generally, stand-hunting techniques work better for whitetails, whereas stalk-hunting methods are more successful in taking mule deer. This is not an absolute rule by any means, and plenty of deer are harvested by the alternate methods. However, the fact remains that the whitetail has evolved to hide and thrive within his smaller, more restricted home range over the eastern and northern two-thirds of the country.

The southwestern desert region is more open and appeals to the rambling, migratory nature of the mule deer. Here, the stalk hunter who makes long-range, well-placed shots with a scoped, high-powered rifle, demonstrates the typical technique. These longer shots call for rifles with larger calibers and more long-range knockdown power such as the .30-06. Thus, in comparison of hunting these two species, ambushing works better on the whitetail, and long-range shooting is best used on the mule deer.

The hunter who understands this basic natural difference between the whitetail and the mule deer increases his odds of hunting success for both species of *Odocoileus*. As for the whitetail, as food and water supplies, weather conditions, and hunting pressures change over his home range, then also do his trail patterns.

Often, though, a hunter may be inclined to suspect that whitetail deer have left their home range under these conditions. And, the accusation is sometimes voiced that "other hunters are killing our deer," because the whitetail is so adept at changing his daily patterns. But usually this situation is only showing the white-tailed deer at its best. This evasive nature of the whitetail *is* the primary hunting challenge presented to the hunter.

Whitetails have adapted well to the eastern, northern, and midwestern United States. In these regions, the whitetail lives within a relatively small home range area. Often the deer can be harvested in open break areas between nearby woods and the thickets where the deer bed and seek cover.

Said simply, the whitetail doesn't leave his home range during hunting season; instead, he alters his trail patterns leading to feeding and bedding sites. He may choose other feeding and bedding sites. In fact, in controlled scientific observations in which dogs have been used to run radio-collared deer out of their home range, the deer typically return within forty-eight hours.

Home Range Extension

There are only a few major areas that I know of in which white-tailed deer migrate significantly out of their home range. Or, one could say that in certain cases, the whitetail's home range is greatly extended, usually due to natural weather factors. One such locality is adjacent to the vast Mississippi River Delta flood zone. Here, along the Delta region bordering the Mississippi River, the spring floods overflow into the lowland hardwood forests and drive the whitetails to higher ground. Deer migrating distances of up to twenty miles are not uncommon then. This is one of the best-known occurrences of eastern deer extending their home range. However, this flood condition occurs over several miles of the delta region. Luckily for the fall and winter deer hunters, following the spring floods along the Delta, the whitetails return to their more familiar home range along the Mississippi River during the summer.

There are two other minor situations in which buck deer extend their home range. First, during the rut in fall and winter, a dominant buck does not hesitate to encroach upon his neighbor's property in search of does in sexual heat. During the rut, a dominant buck may follow a doe that is in heat. Second, a yearling buck leaves the social order of the deer family and matriarchal influence of his mother to establish his own home range. Yearling does are less likely to do this, however. Thus, at these two times, buck deer voluntarily alter their home range. Female deer tend to keep a large portion of the home range that they learned from their mother — the bell doe as she is sometimes called.

The matriarchal doe is usually the first deer down the trail as she leads her fawns and any other young deer and other does in her immediate social order. The matriarchal doe is both the boss and the teacher within her sphere of influence over her home range.

From his tree stand, the deer hunter often views the larger, matriarchal doe leading her group through the forests and meadows. Then, tagging along behind — or aggressively chasing should the doe be in estrus — sometimes comes the buck. A knowledge of this generalized pattern is important to a hunter should he be willing to forego all other deer activity in hopes of connecting with a trophy buck.

However, the bow hunter, who typically is able to harvest either bucks or does, may sometimes opt to go for the lead doe. For the trophy hunter, however, all other deer activity is only so much passing traffic to be reckoned with. Thus, especially in predawn climbing when many deer hunters first climb into their tree stands, it is important to know if any deer activity has occurred. If so, it will generally be the lead doe, followed by other members of the family. And, as a rule of thumb, where there are does, often there are bucks on the fringe of the activity pattern. So, a trophy buck may be following, especially during the rut.

Movement Over Home Range

In ambling over their home range, deer usually move from feeding areas to bedding areas. Here, they rest and chew their cud. Deer do not go through this cud-chewing just to while away their time.

The white-tailed deer has a four-parted stomach. The first segment serves as a collecting compartment where food is stored and deer can thus bed out of view of predators. Thus, whitetails alternately browse in meadowlands, small open spaces between forest canopies, or over the forest floor. After browsing for a short time, the whitetail hides in cover hoping to evade predators. Midmorning and midafternoon are usually bedding times.

The hunter, then, who through his scouting can figure out the feeding and bedding patterns over the deer's home range, can greatly increase the chances of hunting success. For instance, during early-season bow hunting, before bucks have lost the velvet covering their antlers, they will sometimes travel in small bachelor groups, or at least in pairs over their home range.

In doing so the bucks will often browse meadowlands during the night and bed up in nearby cover during the day. A tree stand placed along a newly worn trail near the forest border is often a good harvesting zone.

Deer often travel to and from their browsing sites near dawn and dusk. The tree-stand hunter who scouts and finds these trails may be lucky enough to harvest a trophy buck.

Seasonal frosts that kill tender vegetative shoots alter the natural cover that deer use. Following leaf-fall in the autumn, the tree-stand hunter has a much greater view of deer trails below him. Before leaves fall, however, a deer hunter fifteen to twenty feet up a tree has to reckon with the foliage rendered by the shrubs below. These flat, light-capturing leaves which enable vegetative shrubs to grow also protects the whitetail from the hunter's view when he is sitting over deer trails.

This natural protection can work the opposite way, too, in providing camouflage for the hunter. However, decreasing daylength, beginning frosts, and breakdown of chlorophyll soon cause deciduous vegetation to be void of leaves. Home-range cover for the whitetail then changes dramatically. The deer hunter in his tree stand is no longer faced with the canopy of leaves that shield the deer from view. Before leaf-drop, though, it is a good idea for the bow hunter to clear away leaves and other debris, especially small, dead limbs, that may be blocking shooting lanes from his tree stand. Time spent in preparing open shooting lanes is always well spent.

The whitetail is well equipped for wintertime travel over his home range. By that time the whitetail has grown a thicker, gray-colored coat of hair that camouflages well with the leafless, gray-barked hardwoods. Whereas the autumn hunter had to distinguish the whitetail's reddish-colored coat from among similar-colored leaves, he must now spot the deer's gray coat that merges with gray, winter tree trunks and leafless shrubs.

Reduction of Home Range in Cold Weather

Physiologically, deer are slower paced in winter than in summer. Although the whitetail does not hibernate in winter as do some other animals, their metabolism is slowed considerably. Nature has equipped the deer this way for energy conservation. In February when snow is still on the ground and vegetation is at a minimum, the whitetail moves very little.

In fact, during late winter after the rut, a buck may use only ten to twenty percent of his total home range. Instead, whitetails often yard up and simply try to survive the winter while trying to conserve energy on their near-starvation diet. Consequently, brush thickets, cedar groves, and canebrakes all make excellent bedding and yarding areas where the hunter may harvest deer. Most any wintertime home range contains some pockets of brush, ravines covered with honeysuckles, or evergreen trees such as cedars that provide feed and protection from the weather.

Here, in such cover, whitetails stand idle a lot. For instance, wildlife biologists have observed that during winter, the whitetail beds about fifty percent of the time and stands idle another twenty percent of the time.

Trail pattern activity in the wintertime is greatly altered as deer use a smaller portion of their home range. In late winter, food is at a critical premium for whitetails, and energy conservation is important. By bedding instead of walking, the deer conserve more energy in cold weather more than most hunters think.

Wildlife scientists have found that the whitetail burns sixty percent less energy while bedding as opposed to standing. Although deer may walk to keep warm, they lose in the long run if it is a long, severe winter. It is critically important that the deer retain some body fat for slow energy release, and they do this by being much more inactive than we originally thought.

The wintertime hunter who finds these bedding spots over the deer's home range is at a tremendous advantage. Generally, the whitetail's wintertime bedding sites will be in hollows, meadows, and ravines covered with brush. These areas provide a natural shielding from the wind and its increased chill factor. The chill factor created by a raw, cutting wind drives the temperature downward. Thus, these shielded areas are prime sites for deer during winter gun hunts in many localities.

Southern hunters should scout wintertime canebrakes over the whitetail's home range. A ground blind or tree stand chosen within range of these canebrakes gives the wintertime hunter an advantage in killing his deer.

Cedar thickets and other evergreen groves cover the whitetail's bedding and yarding areas in the eastern and northern states. A hunter's wintertime scouting should certainly include these areas. Whereas cold weather and depleting food sources alter the whitetail's trail patterns in winter, trail patterns are often altered in the deer's search for permanent watering holes in the summer and early fall.

Drought conditions in the fall usually signal that deer will be more concentrated around permanent watering sites. Many of these water holes are shown on most topographical maps. Spring and summer watering places often dry up in the fall. This natural drought condition often coincides with the bow season. Then trails over the deer's home range lead to these permanent watering sites. Further, all deer usually drink at least once a day and often stand idle for a while when doing so. Either at dawn or at dusk, deer typically visit these watering sites. This provides a bonanza opportunity for the bow hunter who has already selected his tree-stand site and figured out his shooting lanes around the watering site.

A tree stand placed about twenty feet high and fifteen to twenty yards from these permanent drinking sites may result in a hunter getting both venison for his table and a good set of antlers for his den wall. Even though the whitetail chooses a restricted home range in relation to his western mule deer cousin, the whitetail enhances his own survival by using a small area in comparison. In doing so the whitetail learns the objects well within his domain.

For instance, any new item or object placed within the deer's home range will soon be observed by the whitetail as he walks his linear trails. For this reason any permanent tree stand or ground stand should be constructed before the hunting season begins. The deer then become accustomed to the stand, and a hunter runs much less risk in spooking the deer during the hunt.

Furthermore, the deer hunter who uses a portable tree stand, as most hunters now do, must learn to remain motionless when the deer observe both the hunter and the stand the first time. While moving slowly over their home range, the whitetail deliberately observes all objects as he walks. However, just because a whitetail sees the hunter on stand does not mean that the deer interprets the hunter as dangerous.

The whitetail, for all his smelling, seeing, and hearing ability, is actually half-witted in form interpretation. Thus, the hunter who can remain motionless while being seen for the first time by an ambling whitetail runs an excellent chance in harvesting the deer.

Typically when seeing a new object for the first time, a whitetail will usually stop and look at it while moving his head up and down. Also, the deer may stomp one of his forelegs and move his head up and down. Supposedly the deer is trying to get the object to move. Then, moving slowly over his home range, the deer looks, listens, and checks out all new objects, the hunter included. The important thing for the hunter, of course, is to be prepared in advance. Drawing a bow should be done slowly and noiselessly just as the deer approaches or passes the hunter's stand.

For survival purposes, the whitetail — as the hunter may also do — uses the buddy system, often traveling in small groups. All members look and listen for possible danger. Consequently, the hunter in a tree stand is faced with a real challenge in trying to kill his deer from among this protective family group.

Some hunters prefer to wait for the deer to pass beneath their stands. A hunter may then opt to harvest the last deer in line, which is probably a buck if there is one among the group, following the does. This technique does not always work, of course, since some of the front deer may perceive the hunter's movements even though they have already passed the stand.

Thus, a hunter's discretion and total field experience are called upon in trying to first remain motionless and then to move ever so slowly while sighting in on the chosen deer. Typically, the whitetail will slowly amble a few yards and then pause for several seconds to a few minutes before moving again at a slow, deliberate pace. In this routine, the deer often seem to appear from nowhere and suddenly loom quite near a hunter's stand. Herein lies the terrific hunting challenge. To get into aiming position when you are caught unaware is very difficult, especially should the deer be looking, seemingly, straight at you. In this life-and-death situation, the whitetail has a full bag of survival tricks.

For, even though the deer occupies a rather small home range, he learns to use this small space to its greatest advantage. The hunter must be well placed, camouflaged, silent, and ready to aim quickly upon the whitetails' approach.

Determinants of Home Range

Even though the shape of a whitetail's home range tends to be oval because he runs linear trails, in the final analysis, the range is determined by natural geography, food supply, and cover. Streams, bodies of water, and vegetation are the three main determinants of a whitetail's home range. Deer activity itself also performs a role in the formation of a home range.

Preseason scouting is important to the whitetail hunter when opening day arrives. The more information the hunter has about the deer's home range and food sources, the better his chances for hunting success. The author is shown here checking vegetative species along trails on Skyline Mountain in Alabama.

Knowledge of and familiarity with an area are the natural forces that restrict deer movements. Deer demonstrate a strong attraction to a known area even when it becomes inadequate for life-supporting requirements. Food supply, water, and even cover may become depleted and yet the deer remain — and often die — rather than leave their home range.

In northeastern Alabama, on portions of the Cumberland Plateau, I do quite a bit of still-hunting. Here, on the 35,000-acre Skyline Management Area and thousands of acres in the adjacent country bordering the Tennessee line, large populations of whitetails roam free. Last season more than four hundred deer were harvested and tallied through the game management checking station on this one management area alone. Yet, in this rough terrain, including the rimrock plateau, deep ravines along the sides, and the canebrakes near the bottom, I sometimes walk many hours without seeing deer. Tracks? Sure. Often lots of them.

Knowing where deer feed, bed, and travel constitutes an integral part of deer hunting. The deer hunter who waits until opening day to check the trails has a lot of catching up to do in the early part of the hunting season. Sure, whitetails change their summer and winter patterns, but past research reveals that seasonal sites overlap almost without fail, even though the winter home range is reduced.

In contrast, overlapping of the summer and winter quarters of the western mule deer is usually not typical. The mule deer has adapted to meet the demands of his environment, too. There are points of similarity, however, in home-range comparisons of the mule deer and the whitetail. After establishing seasonal home ranges, individual mule deer also form home-range boundaries not too different from those of his white-tailed cousin.

In his western range, for instance, wildlife biologists have found that after migrating up to eighty miles between summer and winter food sources, the mule deer then settles down into a home range of one square mile during the summer and one-quarter square mile during the winter. Thus, both species of deer reduce their home range in the winter to conserve energy in fighting off the winter chill.

Also, it has been established that individual mule deer preferentially return to the same summer and winter home-range areas. Thus, home-range studies of mule deer once again demonstrate the

Deer use a much-reduced home range in the wintertime. Biologists have found that the deer move very little except between food and cover. Wintertime scouting, then, is of increased importance as the hunter must find where the deer are located in cover near their browsing sites.

importance of becoming familiar with the deer's summer and winter quarters.

For the nonmigratory whitetail, it is especially important that a hunter learn the deer's daily movement patterns. After a hunter acquires knowledge of the deer's home range and feeding, bedding, and travel habits, thus solving the "where" and "when" part of the hunting challenge, it then comes down to the "how" part of the hunt.

Distribution of whitetails over an area is by no means uniform; it usually relates to the location of choice browsing, watering, and cover sites. Consequently, several deer may have small geographical areas of mutual contact over their individual home ranges. And the hunter who finds these high-activity spots is going to be one up when opening day arrives.

Chapter 13

Bucks and Browse

Growth of Record Racks

The recent set of non-typical racks (1982), which is a candidate for Boone and Crockett records, hails from St. Louis County in Missouri. This huge rack from a 250-pound buck gives the urban trophy hunter, especially, a renewed hope in hunting. This rack from St. Louis County, when listed in the Boone and Crockett record book, will break the nontypical rack record that has stood since 1892, proving that record setting bucks still inhabit the forests and meadowlands.

In order to grow a large rack, however, two circumstances must coincide in the life of a fawn buck: good nutrition and good genetics.

Throughout the United States, deer thrive on many different plant species during the four seasons. Wherever deer live, though, they need sufficient food sources containing the proper nutritional content.

Research conducted at Pennsylvania State University revealed the quantity and quality of rations required to produce normal antler and body development in white-tailed deer. In that study, research-

Deer are browsers and nibble on many woodland plants. If agricultural crops are available, deer also browse on them. Many farmland crops are rich in proteins and mineral content that enhance antler growth on bucks.

ers found that deer weighing fifty to sixty pounds required between two and three pounds of quality feed daily. Deer weighing nearly 100 pounds needed about four and a half pounds of good feed each day. And a buck weighing about 150 pounds required at least six pounds per day.

The deer researchers also found that thirteen to sixteen percent protein in the ration fed to yearling bucks was necessary, and that they attained best antler and body growth when the rations also included 0.64 percent calcium and 0.56 percent phosphorus. Yearling bucks on this ration achieved weights of 135 to 180 pounds and grew antlers having six to eight points.

Even while growing antlers, a yearling buck still needs large amounts of protein, calcium, and phosphorous for muscle and skeletal growth. Further, phosphorous is needed for quick energy release in a buck's body when he is running, jumping, and evading his enemies. In short, a yearling buck is still a growing boy and needs his daily squares of nourishment. As a five-year-old buck, however, he will need only about one-half the amount and still be able to grow a healthy set of antlers.

The whole analogy, I suppose, can be compared to a teenage boy who eats all the hamburgers, milkshakes, and pizzas he can hold. However, that is not so for his ol' man. He doesn't need it.

Wildlife biologists document quite well the food preferences of deer. For example, a study from the Mississippi River border area, close to where the recent St. Louis County candidate for record nontypical racked buck came from, shows the following top-ten food preferences for 227 whitetails. The food types are ranked according to the percentages, by volume, found in samples of the stomach contents. Credit for the study goes to: L. J. Korschgen, 1962. Foods of Missouri deer, with some management implications. *Journal of Wildlife Management.* 26 (2): 164–172. page 166.

	food types	*percentages*
1.	Oaks (acorns and leaves)	30.0
2.	Corn (grain and cob)	26.1
3.	Coralberry (fruit and twigs)	9.6
4.	Sumacs (fruit and twigs)	6.2
5.	Lespedeza	4.8
6.	Winter Wheat	3.5
7.	Grass	3.0
8.	Ladies' tobacco (*Atennaria*)	2.4
9.	Forbs	2.4
10.	Alfalfa	1.2
11.	All other	10.8

An examination of these deer preferences reveals that farmers plant five of the top-ten foods. Furthermore, these rations are known to have relatively high protein content in comparison with other possible browse species in the Mississippi River bottoms. Perhaps the feeding habits of whitetails along these agricultural border areas are somewhat detrimental to the farmers' crops, but these nutritious foods do produce healthy deer as attested by the new

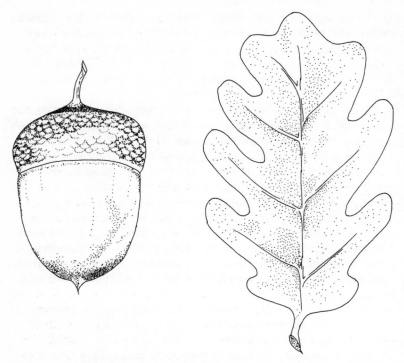

One of the favorite mast crops in fall and winter is acorns. White oak acorns, especially, are sought by the deer. Hunters, while scouting, often look for oak flats in which to place their tree stands. (Drawing by Dixie Holcomb)

candidate (1982) for Boone and Crockett records taken recently in St. Louis County.

Now a point for wildlife managers to ponder: Literature is filled with statements that supplemental feeding benefits a deer herd very little over a long span of time on the large wildlife preserves in this country, especially in the western states. Consider, however, the many border areas in the eastern woodlot regions where many deer hunters do hunt. Many of these urban sections are similar to St. Louis County. Hence, one can make quite a strong case for establishing more borderland food plots in those areas with limited range habitat. Moreover, on many of the large hunting plantations that are now becoming popular, especially in the southern states, mounting evidence suggests that wildlife managers should plant border species that are high in protein. For example, corn, alfalfa, soybeans, and lespedeza are prime preferences for deer.

Mast Crops

Acorns, a natural food source, rank at the top of the list as a wintertime energy source for deer. In a study conducted by the Michigan Department of Natural Resources, penned deer freely chose white oak acorns over those of the red oak species. In that particular study, however, the growth rate of the deer did not differ significantly, regardless of which acorns the deer ate.

An interesting point surfaces in the study of oaks, acorns, and whitetails. The white oak species does cross with other oaks, rendering a variety of hybrids. Whether this is a case of plants evolving along with deer, I care not to attempt answering, but it does raise a point for interesting speculation.

Finally, for a buck to grow a huge set of antlers, good genetic breeding stock is required. In short, well-antlered bucks tend to produce that same genetic trait is their offspring. Sad to say for the trophy hunter, a yearling spike buck will not usually produce a quality rack in future years. In a study conducted on the Kerr Wildlife Management Area in Texas, antler and body-weight measurements collected from white-tailed deer indicated that bucks with less than six points on their first set of antlers (1.5 years old) are genetically inferior. These same bucks will produce inferior antlers for the second (2.5 years) and third (3.5 years) years. All bucks which grew six or more points when either 1.5 or 2.5 years old grew eight or more points when 3.5 years old. Conversely, thirty-three percent of the yearling bucks with antlers having less than six points remained less than six-pointers at 2.5 and 3.5 years of age. Also, eighty percent of the bucks which had less than six points when 2.5 years old again sported less than six points one year later.

The photoperiod, or the length of day that an animal is exposed to sunlight, causes interesting results. As an example, bucks shipped across the equator to New Zealand, in the Southern Hemisphere, alter their antler production to the day-night lengths there. Hence, the bucks grow their racks six months out of phase in comparison to deer in the Northern Hemisphere.

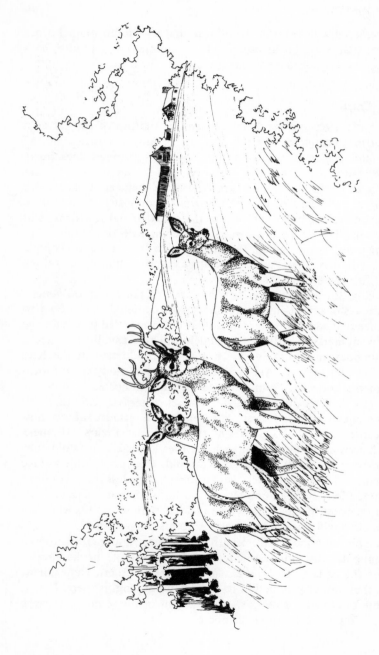

Over the course of the whitetail's evolution, he has adapted to browse and survive near man. Record racks have recently been either taken or found near urban centers, proving that deer can camouflage and hide in woodlot sections near towns. (Drawing by Dixie Holcomb)

The Quest for Bucks

Some hunters seek trophies; some seek meat; some hunt just to get out of the house for their own good reasons—the pleasure and relaxation of solitude, perhaps. But, for the veteran hunter, the quest for a trophy rack ranks high on his list of hunting priorities. And for the bow hunter, for example, the challenge of taking a trophy with "a stick and a string" approaches ecstasy, elevating the hunt to nothing less than a passionate pursuit.

Chapter 14

Carrying Capacity
of the Land

A Correct Energy Flow

Only a certain number of deer can live adequately on any given area of land. This biological limitation is called the carrying capacity of the land. Fertility of the soil, rainfall, and vegetative types — all energized by sunlight and chlorophyll in the leaves — are the limiting natural factors that determine the land's carrying capacity for any species.

Terrain types, whether steep and rocky or lowland meadows, also have much bearing on the land's carrying capacity for the whitetail. Food consumption and energy production by whitetails in wintertime are critical for the deer's survival.

The white-tailed deer lives, grows larger, and survives best in the colder, temperate regions of North America. The general range of the whitetail is between latitudes twenty-five and fifty-five degrees. The whitetail is best adapted for that range because it takes his best characteristics to defeat the colder winters.

However, there is a trade-off to be made: It takes energy to sustain body heat and body functions against the cold blasts of winter.

More deer die from starvation in winter than during any other season. When snow covers the ground for long periods, edible vegetation may be absent. The young doe shown here is fortunate because she is in good condition from ample fall browse. As a survival technique, the whitetail lowers its metabolism in winter. This affects the hunter because deer move much less over their trails in winter.

The whitetail browses heavily during the summer and fall while his rack is in velvet. Later, during the cold-weather rut, he eats much less as he chases after does.

Thus, when the deer herd grows too large for the food supply, starvation is inevitable for the weaker deer. The whitetails, nevertheless, have evolved life-sustaining habits to beat the cold weather. Furthermore, these habits relate directly to the deer hunter and his success. The whitetail just does not move around as much in winter as he does in summer. With radio-telemetry collars, wildlife biologists have found that in wintertime deer use only a small portion of their total home range. This reduced winter activity of deer accounts for hunters not seeing deer on late-season hunts.

Scouting then becomes of magnified importance for a hunter during winter. Wintertime scouting is one of the most overlooked, yet important parts of a successful deer hunting season. Erroneously, hunters think that deer react to cold, winter weather by walking to keep warm. Instead, the deer conserve their energy in cold weather by moving less.

The whitetail has developed seasonal eating habits in order to survive the winter. Deer have adapted to eat much more in summer and fall to pack on body fat for cold-weather reserves. Importantly, though, the fat is not deposited in his muscles. These are kept fat-free and strong for running and jumping in evading his enemies. So, fat is deposited along the deer's backbone, with a little around the kidneys, liver, and heart.

Whitetails then go through seasonal weight gain and loss as a survival adaptation. From December through March they gain practically no weight and more often lose it, especially if the weather is rough and demanding.

Carrying capacity represents an energy flow, upward from the soil and through the bodies of the deer. All land has its physical limitations on vegetative production; only so many grasses, forbs, shrubs, and trees with low-growing branches become available to the deer. Under starvation stress, a browse line is detected on shrubs and tender shoots of trees where the starving deer have shredded the plants. With their lower teeth and upper lip pad, the deer nibble and tear at the vegetative ends.

Under adequate food conditions, deer browse marks are less obvious. But browse marks showing on seasonally preferred deer foods should always be looked for while scouting. These marks are seldom obvious to the untrained eye, since deer browse on mostly the tips of the plants. However, on close observation, a hunter soon learns to look for the chopped tips of twigs, shoots, and leaves.

Attitude of Hunters and Antihunters

Ironically, both hunter and antihunter misconceptions can directly decrease the overall deer numbers by first causing over-population cycles. For instance, antihunting attitudes that are totally adhered to can cause rhythmic cycles in the number of deer on any acreage. With no hunting permitted at all, the deer population continues to rise until gross starvation and massive die-offs occur.

Warnings of such die-offs first become noticeable in small, emaciated deer infected with parasites. Emaciated does exhibiting fawn loss, often up to one-half of those born, signal the onset of die-off conditions. However, the whitetail is physiologically made to withstand certain ravages of nature, including some less-than-adequate diets.

But should deer reach this depleted, emaciated condition and winter is unduly severe, critical die-offs unmercifully cut the herd population. Unfortunately, with many herd members in poor condition, the die-offs cut the population back far below the actual carrying capacity. This is the tragedy that is seldom seen by the antihunting advocates. In short, it is only a fact of whitetail deer existence that the breeding potential, in the long run, always tends to override the food supply on any given acreage plot.

Well-meaning hunters can sometimes add to the die-off problem through their misunderstanding about the harvesting of does. Game management policies may very well change annually on game plots within any state. Thus, the harvesting of does is necessary in order to control herd dynamics and ultimately overpopulation.

Game managers often control the number of does through muzzleloader hunts. On the typical muzzleloader hunt, either-sex deer are considered fair game. Even though the harvesting of a yearling doe may not be as challenging and glorious as taking a wily, seven-year-old twelve-point buck, it is just as necessary for proper game management.

The harvesting of does is often debated among deer hunters. Furthermore, the issue is aggravated because it has crept into deer hunting folklore, literature, and tradition. Under present-day game management policies, muzzleloader hunting provides an effective management technique rendering much sport for deer hunters. Primitive hunting with a muzzleloader adds to the sport because the hunter gets only one shot and then has to reload. The hunter soon learns to make his shot count, and this is in keeping with good hunting philosophy for making a clean harvest.

A muzzleloader is plenty accurate and effective in harvesting deer. Consequently, a relatively large number of does are typically harvested during muzzleloader hunts. Statistically, then, game managers rely on either-sex muzzleloader hunts to thin the herd, especially does, and help to hold the deer population below the carrying capacity, where it should be for maximum whitetail production. Through such planned wildlife management techniques — using the hunter as the proper harvester — a die-off seldom occurs. So, over time, many more deer are permitted to live on any given acreage because the land is used more effectively; its productivity is not overly taxed by browsing.

The Hunter as Herd Regulator

Finally, then, the hunter's best answer to the question of whether or not does should be harvested depends upon what the deer herd needs during that particular season in way of population control. Scientific research on the white-tailed deer has made tremendous strides over the last twenty years. Particularly in the Northeast, Southeast, and the Midwest, several major universities, privately endowed institutions, and state agencies have made significant contribution to our understanding of herd dynamics, carrying capacities, and physiology of the white-tailed deer. The one critical ingredient that must be considered to make the whole system work, however, is the hunter. For it is the hunter's skill, effort, and money that makes game management plans work to peak proficiency. In contrast to proper scientific herd control through hunting, both the antihunter's misguided, even if well-meaning, intentions and the hunter's oversentimentality through tradition can foul the system and not permit maximum production of the whitetails.

More and more, game biologists are planting food plots on many deer preserves. This management technique alters, somewhat, the natural carrying capacity of the wilderness area. Moreover, food plots serve as break areas where deer alternately feed and bed nearby. Especially during wintertime when natural vegetation is depleted, food plots figure into energy reserves for the deer herd.

Once started, however, the energy resources available in food-plot areas have to be accounted in total energy resources available to the deer. Furthermore, harvest numbers have to be taken into consideration. In winters of poor mast production, however, food plots may well serve as stop-gap measures to tide herd members over until spring greening begins.

Food-plot break areas then become prime locations for the tree stand hunter, especially the late-season bow hunter. Typically, trail patterns during this time of season are ever-changing as the deer experience increased hunting pressure. Further, the deer quickly

Garren McBride checks a hillside bench for whitetail signs. Irrespective of their numbers, deer react to hunting pressure, especially late in the season after many hunters have stalked the woodlands. Late-season scouting, however, may still enable the hunter to harvest his deer.

learn to feed mainly at night, and may show the hunter only fleeting opportunities during a few minutes at dawn and at dusk as they alternate trails.

Looking for alternate trails, droppings, browse sign, beds, and tracks, then, in this specialized situation becomes almost a daily necessity for the serious bow hunter. Either actual visual scouting, sometimes at odd hours in freezing weather, or commercial trail counters are necessary to figure out the whitetail's pattern when he is pressured late in the hunting season. This life-and-death struggle for the whitetail shows the deer at his adaptive best.

Hunter skill, patience, time, equipment, and physical resources are then drained and tested by the whitetail's adaptive ability. Gone, then, is the unsuspecting manner in which a deer walked his warm-weather trails. Now, the whitetail just becomes more wary and less obvious as the hunting pressure increases with, usually, falling wintertime temperatures. The season often ends with only the most ardent, dedicated hunters willing to make the personal and physical commitments in stalking or waiting on stand for this elusive prey.

The carrying capacity is a relative number depending upon final vegetative productivity of the land. Also, unpredictable forces of nature, such as long-range but periodic droughts, ice storms, temperature extremes, wind-chill factors, snow depths, disease, and poor mast crops cannot always be controlled, even with the best management policies and hunter harvest.

No section of the country is exempt from deer population cycles, even though the critical, natural causes differ in geographical areas. For example, seasonal droughts occur in the Southwest more often than in the Northeast and Southeast. In the central part of Texas, the state with the highest whitetail population, a severe drought persisted from 1950 to 1956. Then deer numbers declined to the low of sixteen deer per one hundred acres in 1957 when the drought ended. Normal rainfall occurred from then through 1961, and the deer population increased steadily to a peak of twenty-six deer per 100 acres in the fall of 1961.

The following January, this same deer herd suffered a loss of seven deer per 100 acres, as determined by actual carcass counts, when a freezing rain coated all vegetation. Falling temperatures, which then held below freezing, cut off all food resources to the deer.

As wildlife biologists studied this Texas white-tailed deer herd, they learned, however, that the deer population during the 1963 census was back to twenty-six deer per 100 acres, the same as in 1961. The reproductive rate of the deer population, as indicated by the number of fawns per 100 does, increased from forty-two in 1961 to 101 in 1962. Thus, it appears that when a deer herd suffers starvation conditions, the does respond by dropping fewer fawns. In this example, fifty-eight percent of the does did not fawn at all in 1961.

A deer track shows that a deer was once there. After a snowfall, many hunters prefer to stalk-hunt rather than to stand-hunt.

In another regional example, state and federal records show that fifty major white-tailed deer die-offs occurred in the Southeast between 1890 and 1958. Also, it is known that over-population of whitetails in Michigan sometimes leads to the starvation loss of 70,000 to 100,000 deer in a severe winter.

It has been demonstrated by wildlife biologists that in the fall, after the whitetail has fattened, he voluntarily reduces his food intake. This occurs even when experimenters provide tamed or penned deer with ample food.

Deer hunting is a highly individual sport depending on each hunter's quests and motives. Luckily for the hunter, game management policies over the last thirty years have placed about 25 million deer within the United States. That number has grown from the 500,000 deer inhabiting the country during the early part of the century.

Best of all, though, hunting provides an opportunity to engage in a delightful, physical, and challenging sport. The physical exertion of coaxing a tree stand up a tree is not only what many active outdoorsmen need but crave. Sitting there, alone, observing nature, one finds deer hunting enjoyable, contemplative, and relaxing.

In a real sense then, the deer hunter with bow, muzzleloader, and rifle corresponds with three admirable forerunners: the American Indian, the New England colonist, and the western frontiersman. Further, deer hunting represents something basic and necessary to our own existence. It harks us back to our own evolution when we hunted for survival's sake. Too, those drives still remain within us, promoting our future survival.

In providing places to deer hunt, forested areas are important in our society. To receive the maximum returns for both the hunter and his whitetail quarry — the predator and the prey — correct game management and ethical hunting are called for; the first one is relative, but the latter one is not because it involves fair-chase principles. Consequently, in carrying out sound game management policies and in holding the deer population below the critical carrying capacity, should herd estimates show that definite numbers of deer of both sexes need to be reduced for the good of the herd, it is only merciful to do so.

Regulation of deer herds should maintain their numbers below the maximum carrying capacity of the land. This practice allows a buffer zone if unexpected natural disasters such as droughts, food shortages, or deathly wintertime temperatures encroach upon the whitetail herd. In following these policies, individual bucks are larger and better-racked for the trophy hunter. Further, the bucks' offspring can better provide for future hunting.

Chapter 15

Whitetail Adaptability

Survival Through Adaptability

If any singular word describes the white-tailed deer, that word is adaptability. In its whole being the whitetail is adaptable—in its genetics, its physiology, and its behavior.

All of these adaptive traits are applied directly against the hunter in the field. When under environmental, predatorial, or hunter pressure, the whitetail is remarkably tough, smart, and resilient in his defensive actions.

Physiologically, the whitetail has the digestive ability to overcome conditions that would starve domesticated cattle. When it comes to nibbling on twig tips, the whitetail is without peers. Thus, in wintertime the deer usually makes it. Over hillsides, hollows, fencerows, swamps, cedar groves, coniferous thickets of spruce and pine, meadows, or farmland, the whitetail has adapted for survival.

Further, even though deer can utilize and grow fat upon the farmer's alfalfa and soybeans, the whitetail does not prefer such handouts exclusively. In fact, even though deer will include man's food plots in his home range, especially during winter, the whitetail

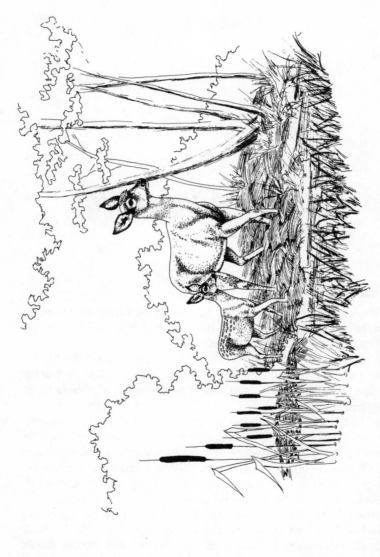

The doe teaches her fawns to be evasive. The wild nature so necessary for long-range survival is taught to each generation of young deer by the does. (Drawing by Dixie Holcomb)

is basically still a browser, a nibbler, by preference, and not a grazer. This means that the whitetail evolved in the nearby woodland independent of man's domesticating and agricultural efforts.

Members of *Bovidae*, the cattle family, developed as grazers. They fit much better into man's domestication plans than do members of the deer family *Cervidae*.

Since deer evolved as woodland browsers instead of grazers, then generally this has exempted the whitetail in the past from man's large-scale domestication efforts. Non-domestication has enhanced the whitetail's wild, evasive nature, but not the hunter's success in fooling this wary creature. However, since the whitetail is highly adaptable, it can be tamed.

Too, deer are highly individualistic. That is a part of their overall adaptability as an animal species. This high individuality among deer is also the reason that hunters may observe certain whitetails making all sorts of behavioral responses in the field.

The genetic potential and physical inclinations for wilderness survival are innate within a young fawn, but it is the young fawn's dam that first awakens, cultivates, and hones these survival skills in her offspring.

In short, the doe, if wild herself, teaches her fawn to be wild. She teaches the youngster to run, hide, camouflage, to nibble on many kinds of woody plants quickly and then bed, to sense the air currents for predators, to startle, or to stand stolid sometimes while an unsuspecting hunter walks on by.

In my interests in researching and hunting the white-tailed deer, I have observed individual whitetails ranging all the way from completely tame to completely wild. Whichever behavioral response any certain deer exhibits, though, one must go back to shortly after its birth for part of the answer.

In order to receive immunity from diseases, immediately at birth a young fawn should be nursed, licked fore and aft, nuzzled and cared for by its mother for a day or two at least.

For whitetail survival, the wild nature and responses must be learned quickly and effectively in detecting and interpreting sounds, scents, and predatorial shapes and motives.

It's a unique experience to walk up to a huge, tamed buck and examine his antlers while they are in velvet. Too, while you are hunting, it is not a unique experience but a disheartening feeling to catch only a rear glimpse of a big-racked, wild buck as he heads for parts unknown.

A wild whitetail's ability then in sensory perception and interpretation impacts directly upon the deer hunter. As hunters we know that should a whitetail see, hear, or especially smell us walking through the woods, then the deer is likely to resort to his evasive tactics. And we will likely never know that the deer was there.

In short, the whitetail is constructed inwardly and outwardly for evasion should his survival situation warrant it. The deer's perception of danger, then, is what sets the wide range of environmental factors that cause him to run. The hunter's abilities that enable him to cover his scent, remain motionless and quiet, and ultimately not be heard, seen, or smelled place him well on his way to getting close to a wild, wary whitetail.

Modification of Whitetail Behavior

There are many grades to the whitetail's startle responses upon seeing, hearing, and smelling man and other potential enemies. In farming areas deer do become somewhat accustomed to the farmer and his machinery. Further, members of whitetail herds may exhibit less of their wild nature through association with other human activity.

The most dramatic large-scale example of this semi-tame yet partially wild behavior that I have seen is in the foothills of the Smoky Mountains. Here, nearly within eyesight of Mount LeConte and Mount Mitchell, two of the highest mountain peaks east of the Mississippi River, the whitetail is flourishing in Cades Cove.

Cades Cove is a vast long valley and a refurbished pioneer community nestled among these Appalachian peaks about thirty miles from Gatlinburg, Tennessee. The National Parks Service oversees the activities in Cades Cove. About 3 million visitors are enticed to the Gatlinburg area annually, and many of them drive through Cades Cove to the wilderness and early pioneer atmosphere. An eleven-mile National Park road winds visitors through this breathtaking area, where cold, trout streams flow from the adjacent Smokeys through several miles of highland pastures.

In Cades Cove the whitetail herd has found a veritable blue and green paradise upon earth in mountain streams and abundant food.

As a result several hundred deer periodically browse over this high-land pasture region. Here, individual deer behavior can be observed and studied. However, even though the deer are protected and free from human danger, they still exhibit their wild, daily patterns. For example, most of the deer browse over this mountain valley only near dawn and dusk. Some, however, may be seen near noon close to the woodland break areas.

Thus, the whitetail here in Cades Cove shows all the wild survival responses but, for several of the deer in the wild, the evasive response has less intensity. For example, some of the whitetails will permit a person to walk within a few feet of them, provided that he/she moves slowly. Other of the deer run should they see you a quarter of a mile—not unlike the true wild state. So, just about every grade of whitetail evasion may be observed here in several hundred whitetails.

Obviously, many of the deer in Cades Cove have had individual experiences with the visitors. Some visitors want to photograph the deer; some children want to touch them; but in all of my observations, no hunting or harsh responses, to my knowledge, have been made toward the deer by the public. No hunting, of course, is strictly enforced by the park rangers. But to avoid overpopulation, the park rangers do live-trap some of the deer and transport them to other herds. My guess is that when this is done, many of these live-trapped deer from Cades Cove develop more of their wild nature, quickly, when placed with a herd separated from so many people.

Finally, modification of deer behavior involves the whitetail's ability to learn. No veteran deer hunter has to be told that when hunting pressure is applied to members of a deer herd, seemingly most of them wise-up real quickly. Then the hunter must fine-tune his scouting. Too much time spent on stand after a pattern has dried up can be wasted effort—even if you do exhibit great human virtues in freezing, sleep deprivation, starving, or any other self-inflicted discipline. But, to know which of these two efforts to engage in for best deer hunting results require considerable field experience.

Concept of Fair Chase

The evident modification of deer behavior in the future as people and deer mingle does have implications toward the challenging

sport of hunting. It is entirely possible now on enclosed game preserves to artificially inseminate does, to entice the bucks with protein and carbohydrate supplements, and to collect record racks in
trophy management of tamed deer. However, that would not only
be a degradation of the sport but also repulsive to anyone who
professes to be a sportsman. Any racks displayed that were taken
under those conditions would be more a display of the hunter's
ineptness rather than his skill. In short, the whitetail deserves better
than to be treated and harvested as beef cattle.

Luckily for the sport of deer hunting, ethical hunters demand
that a buck be harvested under fair-chase conditions. Thus, the
acquisition of a trophy is relative. Certainly, size of rack is not the
sole criterion for which the hunter should be proud. The conditions
and rigors of the chase are the important evaluators that cause a
welling of pride within the breast of the hunter.

Deer hunting, finally, is a life experience, not just a life-taking of
the deer. Consequently, the many early risings, predawn treks into
the wilderness, the pitting of one's skill against the most wary of
large game animals, and lastly, the harvesting of one's meat or
trophy with honest sweat is a tribute to both the whitetail and the
hunter.

The white-tailed deer is adaptable because of his highly variable
genetics. To demonstrate this, let's look at what has been discovered
about the deer's evolution. I once attended a seminar about the
whitetail at a university, attended by biologists and deer hunters
from across the United States. Near the beginning of the seminar, a
well-qualified biologist reviewed the evolution of the whitetail as
shown by fossil evidence.

"The white-tailed deer evolved from a porcinelike ancestor which
stood about eighteen inches high," quoted the scientist. Now, por-
cine means piglike.

Piglike! Then, the full significance hit my mind: The white-tailed
deer, that beautifully constructed, graceful creature that inhabits
North American woodlands, has evolved from a pig. Then, as a
research biologist and deer hunter myself, after thinking about the
matter, I critically considered the general similarities between these
two present-day animals.

Specific similarities still include the split hoof; short body hair;
short tail; similar vocal sounds (both animals grunt, snort, and

make high-pitched sounds); modified, tough, fleshly mouth part (a snout on a pig versus a tough pad on a deer); a compact body; a sometimes short tusk-tooth resembling a boar's tusk grown from the deer's lower jaw; an elongated head; varied diets; the ability to smell fungi and use it for food from over the forest floor (in Europe pigs are used to smell out truffles); no profuse sweating during physical exertion; the general intolerance of both animals to heat; multiple births; similar lower-leg design except that the deer's is much elongated; similar habitat requirements; and both are and have been for many years high-protein sources for predators.

Down through the years, predatorial pressure and harsh winter weather have been the major selective factors in nature that have honed the modern-day whitetail into the elusive and physiologically tough animal that it is. A whitetail is also biologically tuned to overcome the adversities encountered in nature, even on a day-to-day basis.

To begin with, a buck deer has evolved to breed only during the rut, which is generally near the winter solstice: the shortest, coldest time of year. Timing, then, in breeding gives a survival edge to the whitetail's perpetuation. Since the buck can only breed for a few weeks during the fall and winter, it is critically necessary that fertile does are easily detected by him at that time.

Too, the whitetail has evolved to use and depend upon components from the natural world around him: the wind, sun, moon, terrain, vegetation, rainfall, and temperature. Since these components of the natural world have borne and bred the whitetail, then it should be no mystery to the hunter that the present-day deer is an ace at manipulating these against all predators.

Whitetail Research

The reason for the whitetail's great field adaptability, elusiveness, and physical durability has been shown in biological research. Biologists at the Southern Regional Ecology Laboratory (SREL) near Aiken, South Carolina, have studied the whitetail deer for nearly twenty years. Part of that research includes the electrophoretic analysis of animal proteins. In this procedure, animal tissues (proteins) are dissolved in small quantities in the laboratory and subjected to an electrical field applied by a protein-separating unit.

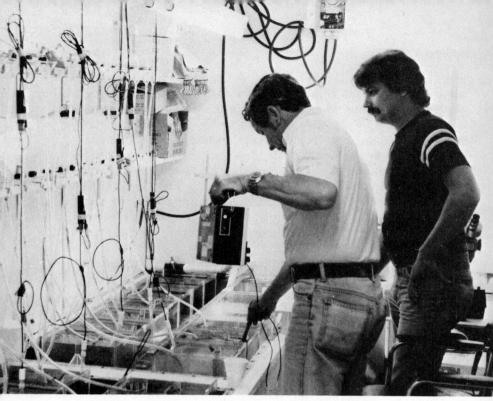

Biological researchers and game managers have helped reestablish the white-tailed deer and other wild game. Here, two Tennessee Valley Authority (TVA) biologists are shown working on an acid-rain problem in the lower Appalachians. Defoliated vegetation lessens the carrying capacity of the land for deer.

Proteins in solution are charged chemicals carrying minute positive and negative charges. Thus, when the proteins are subjected to a direct current, they are divided into discrete thin bands that, when dyed, can be compared for overall protein similarities. In short, this protein analysis enables scientists to study the evolutionary kinship of closely related animal and plant species as the scientists compare protein-banding patterns.

By this means, then, the researchers have compared the white-tail's proteins with that of other warm-blooded animals. All animal proteins are directly formed from each individual's deoxyribonucleic acid (DNA), mutated, changed, and thus evolved over time by cosmic radiation from the sun and contained within the chromosomes of the sperm and egg received from each parent. This all goes to say that the whitetail's genetic material has been shown to be the most variable of any warm-blooded animal checked to date.

Herein, then, lies the secret to the whitetail's great field adaptability to the hardships of nature. In other words, over evolutionary time as the selective pressures from nature act upon the broad range of variable whitetail characteristics, those individual deer that are the best adapted to dealing with the selective forces survive better on the average than other deer. So, by natural selection, those whitetails with internal and external characteristics that promote long-range survival will then become more numerous as more of those individuals live and breed.

Let's look then at some other characteristics that promote sur-

Deer are well adapted to run, hide, or camouflage. Moreover, they seem to know which evasive tactic is called for. Harvesting a wily white-tailed buck is the ultimate challenge in big-game hunting. (Drawing by Dixie Holcomb)

vival of the white-tailed deer. Many of these impact the hunter by enabling the deer to evade him.

The first obvious natural adaptation that whitetails have is their running and jumping ability promoted by long legs and fat-free voluntary muscles. Although a whitetail's legs are long and seemingly delicate, in cross-section the leg bones are robust and thick and permit their durability in absorbing shock when bounding over objects six feet high.

The whitetail then has evolved muscular agility for short, fast bursts of speed which carry him over rocks, logs, and ravines within his home range. Although a whitetail has developed long legs for jumping, his body is quite robust and plumb-bob shaped. This is an evolutionary adaptation that renders a compact body mass for wintertime survival. The whitetail, then, is not really a long-distance runner in the sense that some of his canine predators are. For this reason, dog packs can be a real hazard to deer.

Luckily for the whitetail, though, what he cannot outrun he can hide from. So, from top to bottom and front to back, a whitetail evolved great camouflaging techniques. Branched antlers and long legs blend well with saplings and shrubs. Further, the whitetail's summer and winter coats blend well with seasonal foliage and tree bark. Typically, in summer and early fall, his reddish hair merges with the amber-colored, growing shrubs and tree trunks. Later, fall hues of red and brown fade to drab gray and finally wintertime black. But by that time the whitetail has changed, too. Now, in his wintertime gray coat, appearing even darker in a misty rain, his footfalls muffled by the moist leaves, a deer may walk right under a tree stand before the hunter sees the deer.

Moreover, for the hunter twenty feet up in a tree stand, to see a deer while looking at the back of the deer standing fifty yards away among gray-colored rocks is not easy at first glance.

The evolution of antlers on bucks has served the deer family well down through time. Rack display is involved in establishing dominance within bachelor groups, whether the bucks ever actually fight or not. Antlers, generally, are an indication of the buck's overall health and breeding fitness for wintertime purposes.

The racks have summertime purposes, too. When covered with sensitive velvet and with blood flowing through them, the tender

Much of a buck's actions, routine, and adaptability relate to his antlers. This buck is shown in velvet during late summer while the doe is still caring for her fawns. A little later in the fall and winter, the buck's rack will figure heavily in his dominance within bachelor groups of bucks.

antlers keep the buck a respectable distance from the doe and her newborn fawn that the buck might injure.

Some biologists also think that the multi-divided rack with its blood vessels closely exposed to the air acts as a radiator, a cooling device, for the larger bucks in hot weather. There is a scientific basis for this theory since it's known that deer prefer an ambient temperature of 40 to 68 degrees Fahrenheit. A temperature of 100 degrees in July does tax a large buck's physiological system, especially should he be chased by predators for any extended length of time.

Whether the velvet-covered rack acts as a summertime radiator or not, the buck certainly could not tolerate this sensitive, exposed rack in the dead of winter when the Alberta Clipper comes roaring across the Canadian border and drops the chill factor to 100 degrees below zero. For several reasons, then, it is necessary that the buck begin growing his headgear in spring and finish it by fall.

When nighttime approaches, for visual, legal, safety, and ethical reasons, the deer hunter must clank down out of his tree-stand and call it a day. Then, with flashlight in hand, he winds his way back to either his vehicle or to camp. Just at nightfall, then, is an important and critical time for the hunter in possibly harvesting his deer. Our eyes are adapted for color perception while the whitetail's eyes have evolved for better night vision and movement detection. So, just at nightfall, the whitetail is gaining visual advantage while the hunter is losing it. The hunter then stays in his stand as long as possible, hoping to harvest his deer in the last few rays of light. Finally, though, forms become inperceptible and the hunter must call it a day.

Chapter 16

Our Hunting Heritage

Why We Hunt

Fossil evidence indicates that man evolved in Africa, spread to the Middle East, then gradually migrated over the earth. Much of this migration occurred through survival necessity as early man followed game animal trails. Our prehistoric forefathers were hunters because their own existence and being depended upon the quest, the chase, and the meat obtained. In short, man developed as a hunter upon the earth, and those necessary urges and drives are still within us, supporting our future survival.

In his diet, man is an omnivore, meaning that his teeth, digestive tract, and other vital organs are constructed to handle diets of both vegetable and animal tissue. Man's early diets consisted of a large cross-section of plants and animals.

Slowly through our own evolution, we learned to cultivate certain plants and domesticate some animals. Any in-depth reading of man's legends, myths, and religious revelations show that his own involvement on earth has been intricately associated with other animals. Said simply, all creatures are part of the natural system on earth.

Further, as Shakespeare wrote, "To be, or not to be, that is the question," still holds true in the case of our future evolution and existence. To assure life within the natural system, creatures must be readily adaptable to many environmental changes and natural hardships.

Our own animal species is highly adaptable as is that of the white-tailed deer. Man is so adventuresome in his nature that after his beginnings in Africa and subsequent spread to the Middle East, he tracked across the Bering Straits from present-day Russia onto the North American continent. Thus, man was in North America in the person of bronze-skinned meat hunters several thousand years before arrival of the European fortune hunters.

Columbus, the Italian explorer, looked for a shorter route to India when he floated ashore upon the New World in 1492. So, the bronze-skinned hunters, the first chasers of the white-tailed deer, were suddenly confronted by invaders with new hunting technologies and the domesticated horse.

The North American continent was then a bountiful supplier of game. Historically, the American Indian stalked and harvested the buffalo, deer, and other necessary game for his family existence, on foot and then from horseback.

Many a robust hunter crouched on a limb over a game trail, tightened his bow, and at the moment of release, let a flint-tipped arrow fly toward a white-tailed deer long before arrival of the Europeans.

The French trappers were the first Europeans to penetrate the interior of the new continent as they coursed the rivers looking for game. Further, game was a staple in the colonists' diet as the new arrivals established a toe-hold on frontier territory. This new land, first an English colony, then an independent nation, relied upon animal produce from the land. Then as our nation grew, the call to Manifest Destiny drew the Easterners toward the West Coast. The 1800s then saw the rapid decimation of wild game, not just for food but for irresponsible, unsportsmanlike attraction. Buffalos especially were slaughtered by the thousands and soon roamed the prairies no more.

Gradually, too, the white-tailed deer became fewer in numbers as the frontier moved from the East toward the South and West. Farms sprang up and the wilderness regions became increasingly sparse

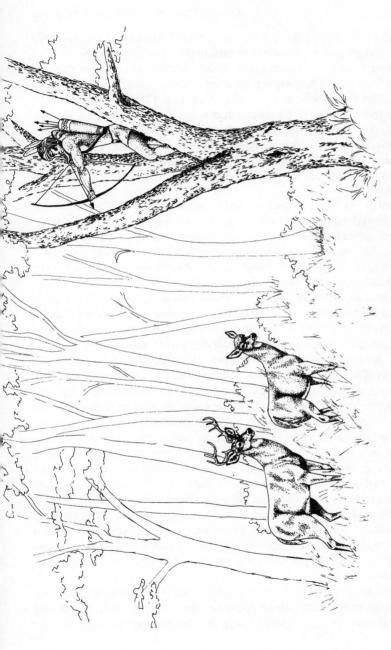

Man, by necessity, has hunted from time immemorial. Tribal people from regions all over the earth have hunted to provide food for their existence. The Indian, as shown here, hunted the white-tailed deer long before arrival of the Europeans. (Drawing by Dixie Holcomb)

with the passing of time. As a result, the white-tailed deer lived only within the inner recesses of the mountains and the swamps.

Such progressive destruction of our natural resources continued until the early 1900s, when it became evident to the American populace that wild game such as the white-tailed deer would soon be gone from the North American continent if not protected and managed. As a result, where millions of deer once roamed, less than a million remained within the whole country by 1920. For residents in some states, a white-tailed deer was only an animal that they read about. In fact, to see a deer within one's lifetime was unusual, indeed.

Following WWII, however, a shift in population occurred as people moved from farms to cities. Technology and agricultural research provided the tools and know-how for better farming practices. Although these agricultural methods were needed to feed a growing United States population, it further reduced habitat for the whitetail and other game animals.

Gradually, though, research and technology provided the basis for the return of the deer. Research and game management showed us how the whitetail could live and thrive in the woodlot sections of our country. Too, some farming acreages were abandoned, as fewer acres were needed and farm surpluses grew through advanced technology. Once-tilled fields were gradually allowed to return to a more wilderness condition, and deer were stocked into these areas by state conservation departments. Reliable game management policies further showed how a deer herd held just under the carrying capacity of the land could be managed with the hunter as the proper regulator.

In the 1960s deer restocking programs began, and slowly the whitetail herds began to return. In the mid-1980s, the whitetail has once again become well established within its original range, with a total population of about 25 million. So, the sport of deer hunting is growing rapidly and gaining new participants. Also, commercial manufacturers make the necessary clothing and equipment for our hunting, and many allied jobs are provided through the sport of deer hunting.

As with any democracy, the people themselves decide their own political preferences which become laws. This is good; it is our strong point as a free people. Into this political arena, however, the

Eddie Evans harvested this fine buck with a muzzleloader on a game preserve in Butler County, Alabama. Under good game management techniques, the hunter is the proper regulator of a whitetail herd. By harvesting individual deer, other herd members survive and reproduce, and the carrying capacity of the land is not overly taxed.

antihunting advocates have appeared. Basically, their point is that hunting of wild game should be outlawed.

Nevertheless, one point is greatly overlooked by the antihunting groups: To outlaw hunting would go against our whole evolution, prehistory, and existence upon earth. Said another way, were we not hunters, we would not be here. Our kind would have already gone the route of extinction.

Also, to understand why the hunting urge is within us, we must first understand the necessary role of an omnivore that is sometimes a predator within the natural order of life. For example, the wild wolf, a carnivore, is a total predator because, essentially, it can eat nothing else except meat. Consequently, over thousands of years, such animals as the northern caribou and the wolf have co-existed, as both are benefitted through the life-and-death efforts of each other. Nature is simply like that. Individual death is a part of life upon earth as time mysteriously rolls on.

Early tribal peoples respected the lives of the wild animals that, by necessity, they harvested. The early American Indian chased wild game for centuries and understood that his life depended upon that game. Historically, then, the Indians as tribal hunters were "killed" when the wild game passed from the American scene. Most of this game was killed wantonly without any thought for the future.

The modern-day, ethical deer hunter knows that poaching and disregard of fair chase have no place in the true sport of deer hunting. Further, any game taken under those conditions cannot be displayed with pride before any other knowledgeable sportsman.

Man's life upon earth always will be fraught with life-and-death struggles. We are, then, capable of killing through necessity, necessity of our own struggle for survival.

Hunting is an expression of our quest for survival. It is necessary in our continued evolution. Moreover, it is a pleasurable pursuit for those animals, man included, that have had to hunt over the eons for survival. Like sexual expression, hunting is a basic, primeval motivator that has promoted our biological existence on earth. In short, then, the accusations of "sex and violence" made against man are, in a sense, true. They are not only true, but in their place, they are necessary for our own survival. However, like all other activities in nature, these two activities taken to extremes render undesirable results.

For example, in all animals, including man, uncontrolled sexual expression leads to overpopulation and consequent reduction in food supplies which ultimately reduces the population. Thus, the natural balances are maintained, even if through the misery of all concerned.

Likewise, hunting and the harvesting of animals has been a necessary part of our prehistory, and it will remain part of our personality drives into the future. Yet through his advanced technologies of destruction, man is plenty capable of "hunting" his own species in great nuclear wars of human annihilation. Thus, the killing expres-

Prehistoric man depended upon meat and clothing that he obtained by hunting. The hunting urge is still present in modern man. This survival urge is best expressed by deer hunting in wilderness areas. (Drawing by Dixie Holcomb)

sion that was, and is, necessary for human survival—as is sex for proper perpetuation—can be abused.

Man, then, as an animal-of-the-mind faces the same biological problem of overspecialization of body parts, as did some extinct animals, should his mind conjure up great weapons of destruction that finally annihilate his species.

These statements are made in the defense of the proper and ethical sport of deer hunting. Deer hunting provides a means for man to express his necessity for a proper meal for his table.

As meat-eaters we have two choices: 1) to go to the local meat counter, or 2) to harvest our meat. In either case the animal is just as dead, regardless of any amount of antihunting, animal rights, or any other apology in defense of our actions. To apologize would be to apologize for our own existence.

Philosophy of Hunting

Man, whether he likes it or not, is placed in the role of a life-and-death decision maker by nature. Thus we are brought to the philosophy of hunting, fair chase, clean kill, and a proper reverence and respect for life, including our own life.

Finally, deer hunting is one of the most philosophical endeavors in which man can engage. Great issues of life are played out on frosty hillsides within wilderness terrain. Adrenalin and sweat flow, and the blood runs hot. Life-and-death struggles ensue, and the game may be taken by the hunter, or it may escape and survive. Such has been the case since time immemorial. Camaraderie, friendship, and competition among fellow hunters are a part of most deer hunts.

The hunter may become lost, fall over a precipice, be mistaken for the quarry, freeze to death, or become overly exhausted. Such are the challenges during the chase. Our prehistoric forefathers faced the same elements and dangers as they gouged with spears upon the hairy mastodons and were, if not careful, trampled underfoot by the charging beasts. But, as a species, our kind survived and carried meat home to hungry mouths. Skins warded off freezing winds blown from receding ice caps. That was a struggle, and when the present-day deer hunter walks down a moonlit trail and climbs

Present-day bow hunters, even with the effective compound bow, still give plenty of advantage to the prey. Bow season in many states is longer than gun season, and enables the hunter to spend more time in hunting.

twenty feet up a poplar tree in the dark, he reenacts that same prehistoric event.

For man's own best self-expression of primitive urges, he needs deer hunting. It permits us to touch the past and to understand from whence we came. Deer hunting gives us a firsthand identification with the Nordic hunter, the jungle prowler, the American Indian, and the frontiersman as we try to gain our meat under similar circumstances.

Much must be said for the primitive weapons hunter who gives more advantage to the prey. The bowman has, perhaps, an accurate harvesting range of up to thirty or forty yards. So, he must wait as the whitetail approaches. The blood coursing through the veins and pounding the heart is the same excitement felt by our forefathers as the moment of truth approached. To miss is to go hungry. Long ago it may have meant starvation; so, the arrow must be well placed to the mark.

Finally, in defense of hunting, and as a note to well-meaning antihunters: Let's not assume that our levels of sophistication, education, or even religion have brought us to the point of stamping out the hunting urge that is within us. That urge is best expressed, even spiritually so, out on a cold mountainside, alone, questing honestly for both food and sport at it has been down through the eons of time.

Index

Note: Italicized numbers refer to illustrations

Some other fine books for hunters
from America's Great Outdoor Publisher

Badge in the Wilderness
My 30 dangerous years combating wildlife violators.
by David H. Swendsen

Grouse Hunter's Guide
Solid facts, insights, and observations on how to hunt the ruffed grouse.
by Dennis Walrod

Microwave Game & Fish Cookbook
Quick, convenient recipes for concocting the tastiest, juiciest, most succulent wild meat and fish meals you've ever eaten.
by Paula J. Del Guidice

Wildlife Management on Your Land
The practical owner's manual on how, what, when, and why.
by Charles L. Cadieux

White-tailed Deer: Ecology & Management
Developed by the Wildlife Management Institute. Over 2,400 references on every aspect of deer behavior.
edited by Lowell K. Halls

Bowhunting for Whitetails
Your best methods for taking North America's favorite deer.
by Dave Bowring

Deer & Deer Hunting
The serious hunter's guide.
by Dr. Rob Wegner

Elk of North America
The definitive, exhaustive, classic work on the North American elk. Developed by the Wildlife Management Institute.
ed. by Jack Ward Thomas and Dale E. Toweill

Hunting Ducks and Geese
Hard facts, good bets, and serious advice from a duck hunter you can trust.
by Steve Smith

Bear Hunting
First complete guide on the how-tos of bear hunting.
by Jerry Meyer

Sylvia Bashline's Savory Game Cookbook
150 recipes and complete instructions for enhancing the unique natural flavors of gamebirds, waterfowl, big and small-game meats.
by Sylvia Bashline

Available at your local bookstore, or
for complete ordering information, write:

Stackpole Books
Dept. WH
Cameron and Kelker Streets
Harrisburg, PA 17105

For fast service credit card users may call 1-800-READ-NOW.
In Pennsylvania, call 717-234-5041.